AFGHANISTAN 101

Afghanistan 101

Understanding Afghan Culture

Ehsan M Entezar

To order additional copies of this book, contact:
Xlibris Corporation
1-888-795-4274
www.Xlibris.com
Orders@Xlibris.com
42441

CONTENTS

DEDICATION

To the widows and orphans of Afghanistan

.

PREFACE

Prior to the Soviet occupation of Afghanistan, very few Americans could locate Afghanistan on the map. The Soviet invasion in 1979 put it on the map. After the terrorist attacks on New York and Washington on September 11, 2001, Americans learned even where Tora Bora was in Afghanistan. During the Soviet occupation when America was not directly involved in Afghanistan, there was no need for Americans to go there and work with Afghans. However, 9/11 changed the situation; and now, Americans and other Westerners are directly involved in nation building in Afghanistan as part of the "War on Terror." This involvement requires an understanding of Afghan culture and society. Who are the Afghans? How do they think and act? Why do Afghans behave the way they do? How is Afghan society different from that of the West?

Afghanistan 101: Understanding Afghan Culture provides a dimensional analysis of the Afghan national culture, pointing out its differences with Western cultures, especially that of the United States, and its implications for working cross-culturally. An understanding of the Afghan national culture is essential for functioning effectively in Afghanistan. While the book is primarily written for Westerners, it would also be very beneficial to Afghan authorities, scholars, and government employees working at the ministry of foreign affairs, and those Afghans employed in foreign firms such as the United Nations and foreign embassies.

This is the first dimensional analysis of Afghan national culture to be written. In fact, it is among the first attempt to analyze Afghan national culture systematically. This work is based on three years of research, observations, lecture notes, discussions, and interviews with Afghans in Kabul and the provinces. Almost all the existing literature on Afghan culture involves a discussion of ethnic groups, artifacts, languages and literature, and some customs and traditions. At best, the existing literature on Afghan culture deals with what I call the *surface structure* of the Afghan national culture. It provides little information on cultural patterns (deep structure).

Cross-cultural trainings usually provide only the surface structure; this is, at least, the case with training programs I am familiar with in the United States. In role playing, trainees are taught how to handle cross-cultural situations properly. But there are infinite situations; and unless the trainees understand the general cultural framework or basic patterns, they will be unable to handle these novel situations. The same is true about the list of dos and don'ts that are provided in such trainings. The trainees are told, for example, not to ask about the female members of an Afghan family without explaining the reason behind it. As another example, they are told that arranged marriages are common in Afghanistan, but they are not given the reason for this cultural trait.

There has been a lack of studies that can provide the basic cultural patterns of Afghan culture; studies that can describe, compare, and contrast cultures for training programs. Afghan languages can be taught systematically because their analyses are available. *Afghanistan 101* provides such an analysis for culture. It provides a framework for Afghan national culture with which a Westerner can compare and contrast these two very different cultural systems.

For Westerners to function effectively in their jobs—military or civilian—it is essential that they understand the cultural patterns of the country they are working in. This book provides the reader with a framework, whereby he or she can analyze and understand Afghan culture. More specifically, it discusses the importance and nature of culture in general and provides a methodology for cultural analysis. In the process, the book compares and contrasts Afghan and American cultures. While the emphasis here is on Afghan and American cultures, other Westerners will find that this framework for the analysis of Afghan culture is also applicable to Iraqi and other Oriental cultures in other parts of the Middle East. Also, the guidelines provided here can be used in cross-cultural studies and training programs designed for Westerners going to the Middle East for business or pleasure. Additionally, the cultural analysis provided here can also assist in the orientation programs for Afghans going to the United States and other Western countries for educational training and travel. Finally, the analytical framework used in this book could also be useful in analyzing the Afghan subcultures, such as the Pashtun, Tajik, Hazara, Uzbek, Turkmen, Aimaq, and others.

Afghanistan 101 is the result of my research and lectures on Afghan culture conducted in the United States and Afghanistan from October 2001 to April 2005. While in Afghanistan, I did research and gave lectures on Afghan culture to the U.S. embassy personnel in Kabul, the coalition forces, and the International Security

Assistance in Afghanistan (ISAF) troops in the capital, Kabul, Bamiyan, and Herat. My lecture entitled "Afghan Culture and Politics" was required of incoming troops to Afghanistan. Prior to my first lectures at the U.S. Embassy, the message sent out called my talk "Afghanistan 101," hence the title of the book.

The feedback I received from these audiences, both in the United States and Afghanistan, was very positive. For example, at the end of one of my lectures to the coalition forces troops in Kabul, an individual from the audience came and said, "I have been in Afghanistan for two weeks, and I wish I had had this lecture the first day of my arrival." My audiences also encouraged me to expand my notes and write a book so other people interested in going to or hearing about Afghanistan could benefit from it.

This study would not have been completed without the support, encouragement, and contributions of some individuals. I am grateful to Professor Geert Hofstede, a well-known Dutch anthropologist who has written several books on culture, for taking his valuable time to read my book and make invaluable comments. Also, I would like to express my sincere gratitude and appreciation to Dr. John Bing, an expert on cross-cultural training, who has taught in Afghanistan for several years and is fluent in Dari and well versed in Afghan culture, for his criticisms and suggestions and for his constant support and encouragement to write the book. I am also grateful to Professor Alice Jach, not just for her comments and criticisms but also for her support and encouragement. My sincere appreciation also goes to Dr. Robert Pearson, an ex-Peace Corps volunteer in Afghanistan, who speaks the language and knows a great deal about Afghans and Afghan culture, for his invaluable suggestions and criticisms. I am grateful to Dr. David Champagne for providing me with the opportunity to go to Afghanistan in 2002-2005 and do the research for the book. My heartfelt thanks also go to hundreds of coalition and ISAF troops as well as the U.S. embassy personnel for their thought-provoking questions and encouraging me to write this book. My appreciation also goes to the Afghans for their assistance during my research in the country. And, finally, I am grateful to my wife and children, especially my son, Waheed and his gracious wife, Geneva Entezar, for their wholehearted support and encouragement. While the above-mentioned individuals made invaluable suggestions and criticisms, I take the responsibility for any flaws in the book.

Ehsan M Entezar
Modesto, California, USA
25 July 2007

INTRODUCTION

I have been interested in culture and cultural analysis for a long time. There are two reasons for my interest in culture. One is that my doctoral degree is in applied linguistics, and there is a close relationship between language and culture. Edward T. Hall acknowledges this relationship by entitling his book on culture, *The Silent Language*. As will be made clear shortly, both language and culture have a distinct structure among other similarities. As such, culture can be analyzed just as language lends itself to analysis. Describing the structure of culture, however, calls for different analytical tools.

The second reason for my interest in culture, however, is practical. From 1963 to 1978, off and on, I was language and cross-cultural training coordinator for the United States Peace Corps programs, both in America and in Afghanistan. For language training, I wrote the first Dari textbook in 1964 at the School for International Training. For cross-cultural training, we made use of "role playing" and a list of "dos and don'ts." In the former, there was a textbook teaching the basic structural patterns of the Dari language. In the latter, on the other hand, there was no textbook to systematically introduce Afghan cultural patterns to the trainees. Both "role playing" and the "dos and don'ts" dealt with Afghan culture superficially and sporadically.

The current literature on Afghan culture, too, deals with Afghan culture superficially and unsystematically. The introductory books on Afghanistan, for instance, deal with Afghan government, history, geography, economy, and so on with culture being only a small part. The cultural part involves a description of the languages, literature, ethnic groups, tribes, and some customs and traditions.[1] Among the cultural traditions of the Afghans, these books mention arranged marriage, hospitality, extended family, revenge, and so on, but they fail to point out the underlying reasons for these practices in Afghan society. In short, neither the cross-cultural training mentioned above nor the current literature on Afghan culture are based on analytical studies to make clear the basic patterns of Afghan culture.

The primary reason may be that, unlike language for which there are several theoretical models, cultural anthropologists have not been able to come up with a method to analyze culture scientifically. This is understandable since the study of culture is the study of man. However, I believe, Geert Hofstede's *Culture's Consequences: International Differences in Work-Related Values* (1980) took a giant step in the direction of making cultural analysis more systematic. His framework enables an analyst to come up with some of the basic patterns or deep structure of his native culture just as a linguist can write the grammar of his native language provided he has the necessary analytical tools. Hofstede's framework is the result of a survey and other studies. In the survey, one hundred people from many countries, including Iran and Pakistan, participated. The participants were all employees of IBM. This book is based on his framework because, as it will be made clear later on, his cultural dimensions are, for the most part, also applicable in the Afghan context and can provide the basic cultural patterns of Afghan national culture.

The findings and conclusions on the applications of Hostede's framework to the Afghan culture in this study are based on many years of research, observations, lectures, interviews, and feedback in the United States and Afghanistan, especially between 2002 and 2005 when I was stationed in Afghanistan. I have also made extensive use of my intuitive knowledge of Afghan culture in this analysis. Just as a linguist can analyze his native language and does not need "informants" or native speakers, one can also analyze his or her native culture. To understand the findings, it is necessary to begin with a brief introduction of some major concepts and assumptions used in this study.

Values

Hofstede defines *value* as "a broad tendency to prefer certain states of affairs over others"[2] and talks about the nature, function, and types of values that are briefly mentioned in this section.[3]

Just as words are the building blocks of language, values are the building blocks of culture. Values are to personality as culture is to society. Just as values shape an individual's personality cultures shape a society's character. Some values are specific to individuals: they distinguish one individual from another (personality types). Other values are unique to a particular collectivity (group or society): they distinguish different national cultures and subcultures from each other. Values specific to individuals and groups form the belief system. Hostede says cultural values are nonrational or subjective because they are learned early in life and vary from individual to individual and society to society. Finally, there are some genetic traits that are common among all mankind and include biological, expressive, associative, and aggressive behaviors. These biological traits are also referred to as *hardware of the mind* as opposed to culture, *software of the mind*.

Cultural values form the system of beliefs, which I call the *deep structure* of culture. This system of beliefs, or deep structure, functions as a filtering mechanism for the surface structure or manifestations in a national culture. These manifestations include feelings, actions, and symbols in a culture. Cultural values involve good versus evil, rightness (*sawaab*) versus sin (*gunaa*), permitted (*hallal / rawaa / majaaz*) versus forbidden (*haraam / naarawaa / ghayr-e majaaz*), clean (*paak*) versus dirty (*kaseef*), beautiful (*zaybaa / maqbool*) versus ugly (*zesht / bad*), moral (*akhlaaqi*) versus immoral (*badakhlaaqi*), safe (*baykhatar*) versus dangerous (*khatarnaak*), normal (*aadee*) versus abnormal (*ghayr-e aadee*), and so on. These values differ from culture to culture. What is clean in one culture is dirty in another. For example, pork is clean in the Western culture but dirty in the Afghan and other Muslim cultures.[4]

Values can be desired or desirable.[5] Desired values are based on the realities of the situation and what people actually do, whereas desirable values are idealistic and based on what should or ought to be desired. This distinction involves the gap between action and words or what people say and what they actually do in a particular culture. As will be seen, there is more often a gap between desired and desirable behavior in Afghanistan than there is in the United States.

Values also have both intensity (relevance or importance) and direction (good or bad), according to Hostede.[6] For example, dating in America is an important aspect of its culture and very positive. In the Afghan culture, on the other hand, dating is not only irrelevant, but it is also considered evil. In fact, in the countryside, an unmarried boy and girl seen alone could be killed by the relatives of the girl.[7]

Culture Defined

What is culture? There are different definitions of culture, reflecting different theoretical bases for understanding or criteria for evaluating human activity: "A way of life for an entire society, including manners, dress, language, religion, rituals, norms of behavior such as law and morality, and systems of belief"; "A set of distinctive spiritual, material, intellectual and emotional features of society or a social group, and that it encompasses art and literature, lifestyles, ways of living together, value systems, traditions and beliefs"; or "The integrated pattern of human knowledge, belief, and behavior that depends on the capacity for learning and transmitting knowledge to succeeding generations; the customary beliefs, social forms, and material traits of a racial, religious, or social group; also: the characteristic features of everyday existence (as diversions or a way of life) shared by people in a place or time."[8] However, for the purposes of this study, Hofstede's definition, based on the analogy of computer software, is utilized in this study. He says culture is "the collective programming of the mind which distinguishes the members of one human group from another . . . the interactive aggregate of common characteristics that influence a group's response to its environment."[9] He goes on to say that some mental programs contain a component of national culture and are acquired from the environment (family, school, and organizations) and others are inherited through genes. Culture gives a society or a nation its identity (character). Within a national culture, there are subcultures as in organizations, professions, and families. Thus, the importance of this definition, as it will be made clear, lies in its direct bearing on how to predict human behavior.

Cultural Norms

According to Hofstede, societal norms consisting of value systems have their origins (sources) and consequences.[10] Nature and man both operate as outside sources in shaping cultural norms. Forces of nature, which affect culture, include the geography (the terrain, climate, natural resources). For example, the harsh climate and terrain of Afghanistan have affected the character of Afghans and how they live. The natural barriers such as rivers and mountains have kept the Afghan communities isolated. This in turn has increased linguistic and cultural differences. This explains why there are so many different languages and dialects in Afghanistan; and how different groups, while sharing some common cultural fundamentals, have their own customs and traditions. Switzerland, due to its similarity of terrain (although not the deserts), has different cultural and linguistic separation of its people although its government is a confederation of its different groups.

Forces of man include conquests, migrations, travels, theories, and technology. The invasions of the region by Alexander the Great, Genghis Khan, and the Arabs, for example, explain the existence of different races, languages, and subcultures in Afghanistan.

Thus, the two outside sources of man and nature form the cultural norms. Cultural norms form the system of beliefs, national culture, or psyche of a people. Norms form the core culture and are shared by all members of a cultural group in a given society.

Cultural norms have consequences in that they affect the surface structure of a culture, namely, the structure and functioning of institutions such as family patterns, social stratification, education, religion, political structure, legislation, and so on.[11]

The Importance of Culture

"Social systems can only exist," says Hofstede, "because behavior is not random, but to some extent predicable."

But he adds that "for each prediction of behavior, we try to take both the *person* and the *situation* into account."[12] Knowing about the individual in turn means knowing about a person's ambitions, strengths, weaknesses, and his or her culture. Knowing the environment (situation) involves an understanding of the current social, political, economic, physical, and other conditions under which he or she operates. Additionally, the more accurate one's information about an individual and his environment, the more accurate the prediction. Thus, to understand the behavior of individuals and societies, it is critical to be familiar with their culture and the current local conditions. Understanding culture, in turn, becomes crucial in how to be effective in the workplace, nation building, and even in waging wars when it involves other countries.

Nature of Culture

One way to understand the nature of culture is to compare it with language as they share several similarities. Language and culture are closely related. Learning about the language, one can learn about the culture. For example, the Eskimos have many words to describe different kinds of snow. This means snow is very important in the Eskimo culture. Similarly, Dari and other languages spoken in Afghanistan have several words for different rice dishes depending on their ingredients and how they are cooked. This is indicative of how important rice is in the Afghan culture. Language and culture are also closely tied together in one other aspect. An accurate translation requires that the translator is not only in full command of the source and target languages but also has a complete understanding of the cultures of the speakers. That is why translating jokes, proverbs, and sayings from one language to another is so hard and challenging.

Neither culture nor language is innate. The capacity to learn language is innate, but not speaking of a particular language. Man has to learn it from the environment. In other words, he needs exposure to a language in order to learn it. While there are studies that show language is not innate and has to be acquired from the environment, to the best of my knowledge, there are no studies proving the non-innateness of culture. The similarities in the nature of language and culture suggest that culture, like language, is not innate either.

Both language and culture are learned in childhood. Like language, a child learns the culture at home and it is reinforced in school and the rest of the environment.

Another similarity is that one has intuitive knowledge of both his or her native language and culture. In other words, he learns the rules of his language and culture subconsciously. This is why, unless one has studied his or her language systematically, he cannot explain questions about his or her native language. For example, a native speaker of English, unfamiliar with its spelling patterns, cannot explain why when adding the suffix *ing*, the last consonant of the word *open* is not doubled, whereas the last consonant of the word *omit* is. The spelling rule in English says, if a word ends with one consonant preceded by one vowel, the last consonant is doubled provided the primary stress falls on the last syllable. In the above example, the primary stress does not fall on the last syllable of the word *open*. Therefore, the last consonant is not doubled, even though it ends with one consonant and is preceded by one vowel. Thus, *opening* but not *openning*, and *omitting* but not *omiting*. In culture, too, one cannot explain why the extended family is a trait of Afghan culture. We shall see that this is due to the fact that the extended family is a characteristic of non-individualistic societies such as Afghanistan. As another example, dating is a trait of

American culture but not of the Afghan culture. The former culture is individualistic, whereas the latter is not.

Additionally, both language and culture have structure. Like language, cultural behavior is not random. It is mostly rule governed and has patterns. It is the cultural patterns that enable us to make predictions. A person familiar with rules of English grammar, for example, can predict what the missing word is in "he speaks Pashto and I . . . too." It is with the knowledge of these rules that a person can understand and produce sentences that he has never heard or seen before. Similarly, with the knowledge of the basic patterns of a culture, one can predict how an individual will likely behave in certain situations. For example, I can predict that an Afghan child on a train or bus most likely would offer or accept food from a stranger sitting next to him. Similarly, I can predict that an American in a similar situation would not offer to or take food from a stranger. The former behavior is characteristic of collective or non-individualistic societies and the latter those of the individualistic societies common in the West. An analysis of a culture provides the patterns or rules of that culture. This in turn helps the person understand why people of that culture behave the way they behave, and at the same time predict their behavior in given situations.

Similarly, both language and culture have surface and deep structure. *Deep structure* refers to the underlying rules or patterns, whereas *surface structure* is the manifestation of these rules and patterns. In English, the sentence "go home" is the surface structure (manifestation). Its deep structure is "you go home." Similarly, the deep structure of "the room is being painted" is "they, or someone is painting the room." In culture, too, *hospitality, revenge, extended family, arranged marriage*, and so on are all examples of surface structure or manifestations of deep structure, namely, collectivism.

Just as one can analyze his native language, provided he has the analytical tools, one can also analyze his native culture. The reason is that in both cases the analyst has intuitive knowledge of the rules or patterns. In other words, just as the analyst knows intuitively which sentences are grammatical (well formed) and which ones are ungrammatical (ill formed), he also intuitively knows which cultural behavior is consistent with the patterns of his culture and which ones are not. Grammatical sentences "sound right" and ungrammatical ones do not. Behavior consistent with cultural patterns appears "Afghan" and behavior inconsistent appears "un-Afghan." To illustrate, a native speaker of the American language knows that "he came yesterday," sounds "right," but "he come yesterday" does not. Similarly, to an American, a child not accepting food from a stranger is "American," whereas accepting is not. Thus, the analysis provided in this study is based on the analytical framework developed by Hofstede and my intuitive knowledge of the Afghan culture.

Finally, both language and culture have components or dimensions. Language has phonological, morphological, syntactical, and semantic components. Culture too, has components or dimensions.

Dimensions of Culture

Culture can be studied in two different ways. One can either study the specifics in order to determine the general patterns (inductive) or study the general patterns to identify the specifics of a culture (deductive). The second approach is adopted by Hofstede in his dimensional analysis of culture. Every culture deals with power, ambiguity, individualism and gender that are universal and exist in all cultures. Here again, these dimensions are filtered through the value systems of various cultures. More specifically, Hofstede divides these four[13] commonalities into power distance (PD), uncertainty avoidance (UA), individualism (IND), and masculinity (MAS).

Cultural dimensions have the same meaning in all cultures; they differ from each other in how they manifest themselves. These dimensions provide a methodological framework for the analysis, description, comparison, and contrast of national cultures. The dimensional analysis of the Afghan national culture provided in this book is based, in addition to my intuition, on three years of research, observations, and lecture notes in Kabul and the provinces from 2002-2005.

Each cultural dimension is discussed in its own chapter, which has five sections: an introduction, an analysis, implications, conclusions, and "Food for Thought." The introduction begins with a critical incident, followed by a summary of Hofstede's major concepts related to the dimension under discussion. Most of the chapter, however, is devoted to the analysis and application of the dimension to the contemporary Afghan life and culture. Then there is a brief discussion on the implications of the dimension in the workplace for Westerners working in Afghanistan, especially for Americans. This is followed by a conclusions section. Finally, there is a "Food for Thought" section. The aim of these questions in the last section is to generate further thinking and discussion about the implications of the dimension or various aspects of Afghan culture.

CHAPTER 1

Power Distance

Whoever drinks water from the blade of the
sword deserves it
—Afghan proverb

Introduction

*As an undergraduate student, I majored in English at Kabul
University, where we had both Afghan and American professors.
Of all the American professors, one, Charles Scott, I will never
forget. He was the one we both feared and respected the most.*

*Initially, we were afraid of him. He looked mean and
rarely smiled in class, especially at the beginning, he looked very
serious; and his quizzes and tests were very hard, forcing us to
study more for the course he was teaching. The primary reason
his questions were hard was the fact that their answers called
not for memorization but critical thinking. The Afghan system
of education is based on rote learning with very little, if any,
emphasis on critical thinking, an important aspect of "learning
to learn".*

*The respect came later when we began to see how much we were
learning. He cared about us and did everything he could to help
us learn. Charles Scott was always prepared and punctual and
wanted us to be the same. In class, he wanted us to be attentive and*

alert. One day, at the beginning of his class, one of my classmates, "Noorali" was playing with a rose while Mr. Scott was teaching. He stopped teaching and turned to Noorali and in a soft voice said, "Noorali, does the rose smell good?" Noorali said, "Yes." In a harsh and angry voice, Mr. Scott said, "Throw it away!" From that day on, the students in our class were always attentive in his classes and took his course seriously. With this incident, he established his authority in class. Just as we feared him, we also had a great deal of respect for him. The respect was partly due to his authoritarian personality and discipline but also due to the fact that he knew his subject matter and cared about us. In Afghanistan, good teachers, even at the university level, are also mentors, coaches, and leaders. Doing so requires that they know their subject matter, enjoy teaching, prepare for classes, care for students, and most importantly, establish their authority to create the proper environment for learning. As it will be made clear in this chapter and the next, in the Afghan culture, it is the authority of the person rather than the authority of the rule.

The question of authority is related to the first dimension of culture, power distance (PD).[14] It involves the degree to which the less powerful members of organizations such as the family and others accept and expect that power is distributed unequally. It is the relationship between a powerful individual and a less powerful individual. To put it differently, PD is the relationship between a teacher and his or her students, a commander and his troops, a supervisor and his subordinates, between a husband and his wife and children, all the way up to a king and his subjects, or a president and his citizens.

Inequality can be natural or cultural. By nature, some people are physically stronger than others, and some individuals are mentally more intelligent than others. Other forms of human inequality can be in the areas of wealth, social status and prestige, laws, rights, and rules. Hofstede classifies national cultures into high and low based on the participants' responses to three types of questions related to "a superior's style of decision making, colleagues' fear to disagree, and the type of decision making which subordinates prefer in their boss."[15] He goes on and states that the greater the extent of acceptance and expectation of inequality among the members of society, the higher the PDI (power distance index) and vice versa. Afghanistan was not a participant in the survey, but its neighbors Iran and Pakistan were. That is why Afghanistan shares some of the characteristics of high PD societies such as Pakistan and Iran. The United States, on the other hand, scored lower and belongs to the low PD societies. Put differently, tolerance for inequality is higher among the Afghans than among the Americans.

In high PD societies, according to Hofstede, employees are more afraid to disagree with or challenge their supervisors; subordinates' perception is that the boss tends to make decisions autocratically and paternalistically and that they prefer only consultative decision making. In low PD societies, on the other hand, employees are less afraid to disagree with their boss; subordinates want their boss to make decisions democratically, and they prefer the persuasive style of decision making.[16]

Other traits of high PD societies that are relevant to Afghanistan include the following: parents put high value on children's obedience, students put high value in conformity, students show authoritarian attitudes as a social norm, subordinates value close supervision positively, there is a perception of weak work ethics, bosses see themselves as benevolent decision makers, employees are reluctant to trust each other, and higher- and lower-educated employees show similar values about authority.

Power distance in Afghanistan also correlates with social power, power and wealth, expert power, decision making, elitism, age and charisma, and authority of the person.

How Afghans Cope with Power

Social Power

In high PD societies, social power is coercive, whereas in low PD societies it is persuasive. In Afghanistan, force and intimidation are usually used to establish one's power and dominance. In other words, might is right; one comes to power by the sword and is ousted from power by the sword. Force and intimidation are common at all levels from the family all the way to the presidency.

Historically, rulers in Afghanistan came to power by conquest, military coups, foreign power, or other coercive and illegitimate means. But it is a characteristic of high PD societies the public thinks such rulers are legitimate. This is because generally, force, rather than persuasion, is the language people understand and respect. In fact, there is a saying in Dari that "one who drinks from the edge of a sword deserves to enjoy it (*harki aab az dam-e shamshayr khurad nowshashbaad*)." Some Afghan rulers even get titles such as "conqueror." For instance, Shah Wali Khan, who captured Kabul from Habibullah Kalakani in the nineteen twenties, was referred to as the "Conqueror of Kabul (*Fateh-e Kabul*)."[17]

Afghans are familiar with force and autocracy. King Abdur Rahman (1880-1901), known as "the Ameer with the Iron Fist," was feared because of his autocratic rule. That is why there was law and order during his reign in the country. He himself says, "People [foreigners] say that the ameer rules with an iron fist; this is justified because I have to rule an iron people."[18] He used harsh methods like burying people alive, blinding, cutting off hands, starving and boiling and skinning alive. He even put criminals in iron cages with only salty bread to eat and salty water to drink. The Taliban, too, used some of these methods to subjugate the population—public execution of women and chopping limbs. Even now, the *ulema* (religious scholars) of Herat asked Karzai in late June or early July of 2007 to allow the courts to punish criminals on the basis of Shari'a (Islamic law). Although such punishments violate human rights, in the absence of the rule of law—meaning no one is above the law including the president—such punishments, in view of the ulema, are the only way to prevent chaos and lawlessness in the country.

The point being made is that Afghans do not respect a weak ruler, father, supervisor, commander, or any other person in charge. Disarmament, Demobilization and Rehabilitation (DDR), for example, has failed for the most part in Afghanistan during the Karzai government primarily because, instead of force, persuasion was used. This is why Afghans are still armed to the teeth; the warlords only surrendered mostly tanks and selected heavy weapons, keeping large arms caches themselves. Nowadays when two rival groups or families fight, they use rockets and rocket propelled grenades (RPGs) against each other.

Once in power, a ruler tries to stay in power using any means at his disposal. No Afghan ruler has given up power willingly. A ruler will rig the elections, force or bribe people to vote, or use other deceptive means to keep themselves in power until they are ousted from power by force. Since the death of Ahmad Shah Durrani, the monarchs and other rulers of Afghanistan came to power by force and were ousted by force. In the twentieth century alone, seven rulers were murdered or forced out, King Habibulla (1901-1919), Habibullah Kalakani (January-October 1929), Nadir Shah (1929-1933), Mohammad Daoud Khan (1973-1978), Nur Muhammad Taraki (1978-1979), Hafizullah Amin (September-December 1979), and Najibulah (1987-1992). Zahir Shah (1933-1973), Sebghatullah Mujaddidi (1992), Burhanuddin Rabbani (1992-1996), and Mullah

Omar (1996-2001) were all ousted from power by force but not killed. This vicious cycle of coming to power by force and ousting from power by force has been going on for centuries

Power distance does not just involve the ruler and the ruled: it also manifests itself in the family, schools, and other public and private institutions and organizations in Afghanistan. In the family, the father is the absolute power. He must be obeyed, and his ideas and decisions cannot be challenged. He makes decisions for his family members in marriage, education, and other aspects of life. Disobedience is punished, ranging from verbal abuse to physical punishment to divorce in the case of the wife and disowning in the case of children. Some husbands establish their authority in the early days of their marriage by scaring and intimidating their wives. It is said that a powerful husband should kill a cat (or "cat killing") on the first night of the wedding to teach his wife a lesson. This may seem cruel to a Westerner, but Afghans do not like dogs and cats.

In schools, too, teachers are usually autocratic and "know-it-all." Students are afraid to ask questions in class, and rote learning is common. Teachers, too, establish their power the first time they enter a classroom by yelling, beating, insulting, or using other harsh means to make sure his students are afraid of him and his authority is established.

The same relationship exists between employers and their employees. Some supervisors punish or intimidate the employees working for them to establish their power early on, using such means as insults, transfers, salary cuts, demotions, and even dismissals.

Social power in low PD societies such as the United States is legitimate. Presidents and other government officials are elected by the people. Besides, there are term limits and, more importantly, checks and balances to keep them from becoming too powerful. In short, in the West, social power is legitimate and must be earned, where in Afghanistan it is obtained by force and other illegal means.

Power and Wealth

Another manifestation of PD involves the relationship between power and wealth. In high PD societies, such as Afghanistan, they are inseparable. A wealthy person is also powerful and vice versa. With wealth, one comes to power; and with power, one accumulates wealth. If one is wealthy, he can obtain important posts in the government and get away with crimes and wrongdoing through bribery and connections. This explains why no high-ranking official or major drug dealer has been indicted or put on trial in Afghanistan.

A powerful person is also rich and, if he is not, he will get rich fast. That is why corruption is rampant in Afghanistan, especially now that the international community is donating billions of dollars for reconstruction, nation building, and humanitarian purposes. The idea is to get rich regardless of the means used to achieve it. Corruption is so widespread now that one can hardly get anything done through government organizations.

As soon as a person—primarily men—comes to a position of power and influence in the government, he or she fills his or her (primarily men) pockets through legal and illegal means. The average monthly salary of a government employee at a ministry is between $50 and $ 80 while a minister makes thousands. In addition to his salary, a minister gets $1,000 a month for "entertainment" (*kharch-e destarkhan*). The most lucrative government jobs are at the ministries of interior, finance, judiciary, office of the attorney general, rural development, drug control, and urban development. The ministry of interior appoints provincial governors (*walis*), district governors (*hakims*), and sub-district governors (*alaqadars*). This ministry also appoints chiefs of police and recruits the policemen as well as border guards. The ministry of finance is in charge of customs and collection of taxes. The ministry of rural development spends hundreds of millions of dollars on reconstruction projects. To get a project, one has to pay a commission (at least 10 percent) to the government official. To get a position in these ministries, one has to bribe to get a job. Some of these ministries spend tens of millions of dollars on projects. For example, the ministry of urban development spends hundreds of millions on building houses and apartments, roads, and other types of construction work in the countryside. Obtaining positions in the ministries of interior and finance usually requires strong ties and cold cash, or both. The bribe money paid to the officials pays off later when the newly appointed individual goes to his new job and begins taking bribes and gifts from people. In the other ministries, too, the departments of administration (*edari*) are lucrative because they are in charge of personnel and procurement. In hiring personnel, bribery is involved and in purchasing commodities or building facilities, officials of these departments take commissions. Corruption has always been a problem in Afghanistan. Cabinet members refuse to register their assets, even though it is required by law. Thus, in countries like Afghanistan, one gets rich by holding a position of power in the government. The goal is to get rich, and it is not important *how*.

In some low PD societies such as the United States, on the other hand, one can become rich *after* holding a high position in the government. Some ex-government officials in the United States get lucrative jobs with corporations as board members, executives, or lobbyists because of their connections in the government. Using their connections with the government, they help the corporations in obtaining lucrative government contracts and tax cuts and other benefits. That is why people take pay cuts to get government jobs because it pays off later. Bribery is against the law in the United States. What some ex-government and current government officials do can be called, "legal" bribery. Finally, in the United States, one cannot come to power without lots of money. Presidential elections require millions of dollars. That is why some people refer to America as government of the rich, by the rich and for the rich. But what makes America different from Afghanistan and other high power distance societies is that in the former, there are free and fair elections, and people choose their own government-elected officials without force and intimidation.

Expert Power

Expert power or the relation between power and knowledge is still another manifestation of power distance. Unlike low PD societies such as the United States where knowledge is power, expert power does not carry much weight in high PD societies such as Afghanistan. Here, what matters is *who* you know, not *what* you know. In Dari, this difference is referred to as *rawabit* (an Arabic word meaning "connections or relations") and *zawabit* (principles in Arabic). Consequently, there is not much emphasis on knowledge and expertise in high PD societies such as Afghanistan.

The word *knowledge* does not have the same meaning in the West and in the East. *Knowledge* in the West is defined as "the range of one's information or understanding of a science, art, or technique." In the East in general and in

Afghanistan in particular, it is equivalent of the English word *knowledge* in Dari and Pashto is *elm*, an Arabic word whose agentive form is *alem* (scholar) and its plural *ulema* (scholars). Originally, the word *elm* meant Islamic studies and *alem*, a (religious) scholar. Until the beginning of the last century, all formal and informal education in Afghanistan was restricted to Islamic studies. Religious scholars have always enjoyed social status and prestige; and they still do, especially during and after the civil war in Afghanistan. In fact, at times, these scholars were kingmakers in the country. However, these ulema were also related to Sufi brotherhood with their disciples. The Mujaddidis, for example, are said to have played a key role in the overthrow of King Amanullah Khan and the return of Mohammed Nadir Khan to power in the 1920s and 1930s respectively.

The extended meaning of *elm* also includes the natural and social sciences but not the arts or techniques. Thus, there are religious and secular scholars in the country, the former being more powerful than the other.

The situation of artists is even worse than the secular scholars. Musicians and singers used to come from the lowest classes. Barbers, for example, used to cook, wash the dead, perform circumcisions, and play music in our village, southwest of Kabul City; that is why Afghans generally look down on people who sing and play musical instruments. In the 1960s, one of the popular Afghan singers had to use the pseudo name Nashenas ("unacquainted") because he did not want listeners of Radio Kabul or Afghanistan to know his real identity.

In Afghanistan, generally speaking, a person is usually judged more on the basis of his position of power and wealth than his character, education, expertise, or any other intellectual and artistic achievements. This explains the brain drain in developing countries, most of which fall into the category of high PD societies. Scholars go to the West where knowledge is power and they can enjoy fame, popularity, and wealth. A good example is the Afghan immigrants in the West where talented singers like Nashenas became rich and more popular after leaving Afghanistan for the West as a refugee.

When I went to the United States as a refugee in 1980, I told my children to study hard because knowledge is power there. Experts in America need not have connections to get good jobs because knowledge is power there and in other Western societies.

In Afghanistan, appointments in the government, scholarships, and government contracts and other opportunities are usually based on connections rather than expertise and qualifications. For the most part, ministers, governors, chiefs of police, commanders, judges, ambassadors, and others are often appointed on the bases of political expediency, familial, tribal, regional, friendship, ideological, or other ties rather than their qualifications. What is worse is that sometimes an incompetent official is promoted if there are a lot of complaints about him. This obviously makes the public lose faith in the government.

Unlike in the United States and other low PD societies, in Afghanistan, search committees do not exist to find the most qualified people. Government posts lower than ministers and deputy ministers are not made public, so people can apply for them. Only for international organizations and technical positions in the ministries are qualifications published in the newspapers. Ministers usually appoint their relatives, friends, and fellow tribesmen. If, for example, a minister is a Hazara, that ministry is full of Hazaras, or the key positions are held by them. Similarly, if the minister happens to be a Pashtun, more Pashtuns get the important jobs in his ministry. Government contracts, too, are usually given to those with connections rather than their expertise and history of good performance. This results in not much work getting done, and when it is done, it is usually sloppy. In some situations, lives are lost due to lack of competence and poor performance. The Jumhuriat Hospital in Kabul, for example, collapsed soon after it was rebuilt, killing some people because of the sloppy construction work.

Decision Making

Still another manifestation of power distance involves decision making. In high PD societies such as Afghanistan, decision making is autocratic or consultative whereas in low PD societies such as the United States, it is democratic and persuasive. In Afghanistan, decisions are made either personally or in consultation at all levels of society depending on the nature of the issue. Decisions involving the community are made through consultations. Disputes are also resolved through consultations, especially in the countryside. This explains why Afghanistan is the "land of councils (*shuras or jirgas*)." The word *shura*, used in both Pashto and Dari, for example, is an Arabic word meaning "national assembly" or "parliament." There are other councils as well, such as the tribal councils (*jirga-ye qawmi*), the ulema councils (*shuray-e ulema*), the provincial councils (*shura-ye wilayati*), and others. Many disputes within and between families and tribes are usually resolved through such councils rather than in government courts. The primary reason is that compared to the government courts they are a lot less corrupt, more convenient, and less expensive.

The root of consultation is both religious and cultural. The Qur'an says people should consult among themselves. Counseling is also a characteristic of tribal societies. In the workplace, however, autocratic style of management is more common in the country.

In low PD societies such as the United States, on the other hand, decision making is democratic and persuasive. Aside from persuasion, referenda, polls, and other means are also used to get people involved in the decision-making process.

Elitism and Pluralism

Also, high power distance societies are elitist rather than pluralist as is the case in low PD nations. An *elite* is defined as "a person in position of power and influence." According to Hofstede, "Pluralist societies are less unequal than elitist societies but still maintain large inequalities."[19]

In the Afghan context, we need to make a distinction between the elites in the old political order and the new. More specifically, between the traditional elite that existed prior to the invasion and occupation of the country by the Soviet Union in 1979 and the new elite formed after the occupation and civil war.

Until the Soviet invasion of 1979, according to Olivier Roy, the urban elites consisted of educated middle class people—the Communists and Islamists—who opposed the monarchy but were powerless. The real power was with the Durrani tribal aristocracy and landowners. He says that in the countryside and rural areas, the elites were "made up of the khan, the *mawlawi* or the *hakim* (or *woluswal*)—that is, respectively, a landowner head of powerful local *qawm*; a cleric trained in a high level but generally private, *madrasa*, and the district administrator, an outsider appointed from Kabul."[20]

The Soviet invasion and the subsequent jihad against the Soviets as well as the civil war politicized Afghanistan and changed the old political order. The Western-educated and secularist intelligentsia left the country after the

Communist coup of 1978 while the Communists—Leninists and Maoists—departed after the takeover of the Mujahideen in 1992, thus paving the way for the Sunni and Shi'i Islamists and traditional religious parties to dominate the scene. Thus in this new political order, the elites are primarily the former Mujahideen, the former Sunni and Shi'i traditionalists and Islamists, and a small number of secularists.

The Sunni Islamists consist of *Hizb-e Islami* (Islamic Party), led by Gulbuddin Hekmatyar, known as *Hizb-e Islami Hekmatyar* (HIG), *Hizb-e Islami* (Islamic Party or HIKH) led by the late Mawlawi Yunis Khalis, *Jamiat-e Islami* (Islamic Society) led by Professor Burhanuddin Rabbani, and *Itihad-e Islami* (Islamic Alliance) led by Professor Abdurab Rasul Sayyaf. The Sunni traditionalists include *Mahaz-e Milli-e Islami* (National Islamic Front) led by Pir Sayed Ahmad Gailani, *Jabh-e Nejat-e Milli* (National liberation Front), lead by Sebghatullah Mujaddidi, *Harakat-e Inqelab-e Islami* (Islamic Revolutionary Movement), lead by the late Mawlawi Mohammad Nabi Mohammadi.

The Shi'i Mujahideen parties include *Harakat-e Islami* (the Islamic movement), led by Shiekh Asif Muhsini and *Hizb-e Wahdat* (the Unity party), led by Karim Khalili. In addition to the former Mujahideen, the new elites also include a small number of monarchists, leftists and Western educated technocrats with ties to Hamid Karzai and the former king (Father of the Nation).

Since December of 2001, the new elites, especially the former Mujahideen, have dominated all the branches of the Karzai government. They were also in the majority in the Loya Jirga (Grand Assembly), the Constitutional Loya Jirga and now the new parliament. These elites have also dominated the important current and old councils and commissions in Afghanistan such as the provincial councils (*shuray-e wilayats)*, the election commission (*kumisyoon-e intekhabat*), the constitution draft council (*kumissyoon-e qanoon-e assassi*, the ulema council [*Shura-ye Ulema*]), and others.

Thus, the old elites—members of the royal family, the Khans, tribal leaders, *maliks* (village elders) and some Western-educated Afghans—have lost their wealth and social status and mostly live on welfare in America and other Western nations. They have been replaced mostly by people who, prior to the Soviet occupation and civil war, were very poor with little wealth and social prestige. Many of the new elites who hold important government posts are very wealthy and live in luxurious villas in Kabul and in the provinces. It is important to note that some Western-educated Afghans, who lived in the West prior to the civil war, were given posts in the interim government led by Hamid Karzai and are also part of this new elite. They, too, have become rich and enjoy a lot of prestige and power. It is worth noting that almost all the personalities who came to power during the interim government have maintained their top positions also in the transitional and now in the elected governments. In short, with a few exceptions, the same new elites have been in power since December 2001.

Age and Charisma

In high PD societies such as Afghanistan, old age and charisma are also associated with power. Compared to low PD cultures, the elderly enjoy more respect and power at all levels from the head of the family to the governor of a province, to the leader of an organization to the ruler of the country. The older a person becomes, the more attention and respect he enjoys. Everything else being equal, an elderly person has more social power and prestige than a younger individual. Being religious also increases an elderly person's social power, especially in small towns and rural areas. At social gatherings, the elderly get the senior position, far away from the door. Within a family, the elderly are the center of attention. They provide advice and consultation because of their experience. They also resolve disputes between individuals, families, and tribes. They are referred to variously as *kalan* (elders), *reesh safaid* or *aqsaqal* (gray bearded); a "gray beard" or senior is at least fifty years of age. They are usually chosen as *wakil* (representatives) in towns and cities as well as in councils (*jirgas* or *shuras*) or parliament (*Shura-ye Milli*). Some are prayers leaders (*mullas*), *mawlawis*, and religious figures. These people, especially the Wakils are the bridge between the people and the government. Government officials get in touch with these people to reach the people in towns and villages.

This is also true about the rulers of Afghanistan. Young rulers have not lasted long. Everything else being equal, an older leader lasts longer than a younger one. For example, Amir Habibullah (1901-1919) came to power at the age of twenty-eight, Shah Amanullah (1919-1929) at twenty-five, and Dr. Najibullah (1986-2002) at thirty-nine. They were all either murdered or overthrown from power. In the Afghan culture, a young ruler is not fit to govern effectively because he is considered "immature" (*khaam*), "naïve" (*saadalaw*), "unwise" (*beyaql*), "unwise", "inexperienced" (*beytajruba*), and "boyish" (*bachakheyl*). Mohammad Zahir (1933-1973) lasted for more than forty years even though he became king at the age of nineteen because, for all intents and purposes, his three elderly uncles actually ruled the country for decades; Mohammad Zahir was king only in name for a long time. The next chapter (page 21) explains why Afghans do not trust the young to make decisions.

Charismatic individuals also enjoy social power for their deeds or leadership skills. The majority of charismatic leaders are religious. However, there are also some leaders who are not necessarily religious but have earned the respect of the public through bravery in wars against foreigners or any other national cause. For example, the late Commander Ahmad Shah Massoud, from Panjshir, enjoyed tremendous respect and prestige especially among the Tajiks. It is worth noting that there are few, if any, national charismatic leaders in Afghanistan for a variety of reasons. One is that the Afghan rulers did everything to eliminate potential and real opposition leaders. Another is that Afghan loyalties are local and along ethnic and sectarian lines. In fact, different ethnic groups try to discredit leaders from rival ethnic groups. Finally, in the absence of political parties, national leaders do not usually emerge. This, at least, partly explains why there are no national heroes in Afghanistan, past or present, acceptable to all the ethnic groups.

Authority of the Person

Another important manifestation of high power distance in Afghanistan is authority of the person rather than authority of the rule or position. In this culture, rules are not rules to be abided by regardless of who is in charge. Instead, rules are obeyed only if the individual in charge is authoritarian and uses force. That is why when a new supervisor, for example, is appointed, the first questions the subordinates ask are not his educational and academic qualification. Rather, they want to know if the person is authoritarian and, more importantly, well connected—a well-connected person in the government has close ties to higher ups is powerful. Being authoritarian alone without power to enforce the rules is not sufficient. A powerless person cannot enforce the rules and eventually loses control. This is the case in all organizations from the family to small and large private and public organizations such as the government. In short, a teacher, father, director, supervisor, commander, minister, and even the president needs to be authoritarian and powerful for the rules and regulations to be abided by.

Power Distance in the Workplace

Power distance in Afghan culture also has practical applications for the Westerner working in Afghanistan. The first day of work is crucial. As a supervisor, it is important to state your policies very clearly, making sure everyone fully understands them. Work ethics, criteria of promotions, and performance evaluations need to be explained. Teamwork, willingness to learn (expert knowledge), and hard work are to be emphasized and rewarded. Asking the employees for their opinions suggest that they are participating in decision making. Once decisions are made, however, they need to be followed through. The idea is to establish authority the first day. If authority is lost, it is hard to reestablish it.

It is better not to accept invitations for lunch or dinner, at least during the first three months. Most Afghans are poor and a dinner for a foreign guest could cost up to $100; the monthly salary of a government employee is about $60. Besides, such invitations are a form of bribery. However, weddings and engagements are different. There is no problem attending such gatherings provided they are safe and secure.

Also, it is not a good idea to get too friendly and joke around, especially at the beginning. Afghans often do not make a distinction between business and pleasure. The idea is to establish authority the first day. If authority is lost, it is hard to reestablish it. Finally, as will be explained in chapter three, it is crucial to learn the ethnicity, sect, place of birth and other sources of loyalties of the Afghan employees in the workplace. An understanding of these loyalties explains their biases and tendencies.

As a rule of thumb, it pays off to be firm and fair to everyone and stick to one's principles. This may be hard on subordinates initially, but this is the best way to earn their respect and at the same time make use of their full potential in getting things done. As has been explained, it is important to remember that, in the Afghan national culture, it is the authority of the person rather than the authority of the rule that is dominant.

Whether a supervisor or a subordinate, it is critical for the Westerner to be competent in his or her field. Afghans expect foreigners to be well qualified for the job. For the subordinate Westerner, too, the first three days on the job are very crucial. The Westerner should establish his or her identity and learn about the goals of the firm and ways and means of achieving them. Similarly, one needs to learn the rules and regulations and the logic behind them. Here, too, it is not a good idea to be too friendly at the beginning. The Western employee should get across the idea to the Afghan supervisor that he is well qualified for the job, has work ethics, and is a man of principles who could not be influenced by threats, intimidation, or other means. The perception in Afghanistan is that some foreigners try to "cooperate" with the authorities and close their eyes to corruption and other wrongdoings in order to have their contracts extended. Westerners need to be a model of work ethics, dedication, hard work and honesty, integrity, professionalism, and other positive values of Western democracy. After all, foreigners are the ambassadors of their country to Afghanistan. As such, these values need to be demonstrated in action.

Conclusions

In summary, Afghanistan is a high power distance society where social power is coercive, expert power is nonexistent, decision making is autocratic and consultative, power cannot be separated from wealth, elitism is dominant, age and charisma are respected, and Afghans respect the authority of the person rather than that of the rules.

This has implications for the Afghan government and the international community in reconstruction, nation building, and employment in the country. One is that persuasion alone is not enough to get anything done without using force as a last resort. Another is that unless proper measures are taken, funds for reconstruction could be misdirected, misused, and abused; the close union of power and wealth leads to corruption in the government, especially at the highest levels. Finally, in the Afghan national culture, inequality is defined from below, not from above, suggesting that the level of inequality in Afghan society is endorsed by the followers as much as by the leaders. That is why when the ruler or administrator is weak, people tend to disrespect him and/or disobey the laws, rules and regulations, leading to lawlessness and chaos and even the creation of multiple centers of power. Thus, it is crucial to appoint mature, competent, and strong personalities in the government at all levels, especially in the security forces. It is important to keep in mind that in Afghan culture, what carries weight is the authority of the ruler rather than the authority of the rule that counts. Authority of the rule relates to the second dimension of culture, uncertainty avoidance, which is the subject matter of the next chapter.

Food for Thought

(1) Why are the roots of power distance in the family?
(2) In the authoritarian traditional society of Afghanistan, how do religion and traditions relate to power distance?
(3) When a president, a commander, a supervisor, or a father is weak, what would be the psychological

impact on the citizens, the soldiers, subordinates, and family members? Why?

(4) What needs to be done in Afghanistan so that knowledge becomes power? Does the international community have any role to play?

(5) Do the majority of the existing personalities holding top positions in the three branches of Afghan government have the necessary expertise and other qualifications? Why?

(6) Power distance also involves occupation and classes. Prior to the Soviet occupation and the civil war, the most sought-after career was to become an officer, as the military enjoyed tremendous social prestige, high salaries, perks, and privileges in Afghan society. Now, however, it is almost the opposite. Why?

(7) What are the most sought after careers in the government and in the private sector? Why?

(8) You are in charge of the training of ANA (Afghan National Army) or ANP (Afghan National Police). On your first test, a few trainees fail. Someone higher up in the chain of command calls you in and asks you to pass one of the trainees who happens to be his nephew. What do you do and why?

(9) Are the existing Afghan leaders charismatic? Explain your answer.

(10) When I went back to Afghanistan after twenty-five years, I found the absence of the rule of law and rampant corruption in the government very striking. If you are already in the country, what other manifestations of power distance do you see? Why?

(11) Were the last presidential and parliamentary elections free and fair? Why?

CHAPTER 2

Uncertainty Avoidance

God is the source of both good and evil.
—Afghan saying

Introduction

When I was teaching at Kabul University, I would assign more homework than the other professors and give more frequent quizzes and tests to make the students study harder. Whenever I asked my students if they would do their homework and study for the next exam, they would say, "Insha'Allah" (God willing). This phrase is usually used when Afghans are not certain about doing something, blaming God or another person for not fulfilling a promise, meeting a deadline, or following a schedule. That is why the Westerners used to call Ariana Afghan Airline the Insha'Allah Airline, for not being on time among other things. Religion is one of the methods national cultures use to reduce uncertainty. This phenomenon relates to the second dimension of culture: Uncertainty Avoidance (UA).[21]

Dealing with uncertainty has always been a problem of humanity. UA deals with uncertainty, ambiguity, and fear about nature, other men, and the supernatural. The degree of tolerance or intolerance of uncertainty varies from culture to culture. Some cultures program their members to feel more tolerant of unstructured situations than others. Unstructured situations involve novelty, unfamiliarity, surprises, and so on. Americans, for instance, are more adventurous than Afghans because the former are more tolerant of uncertainty than the latter.

Using three criteria, Hofstede divides societies into high and low on the UA scale: stress and anxiety, job stability and rule orientation. Societies with low tolerance for uncertainty scored high in the uncertainty avoidance index, whereas those with high tolerance scored low. Thus, a national culture is a high uncertainty-avoiding society if it is less tolerant of anxiety. In high uncertainty avoidance societies, employees stay longer on the same job. Finally, more rule-oriented societies are on the high side and those less rule-oriented ones on the low.[22] In a rule-oriented society, people are usually law abiding and stick to rules and regulations regardless of supervision. For example, you stop at a stop sign even if there are no other vehicles, pedestrians or police. Put differently, the more uncertainty avoiding a country is, the higher it is in UA. UA is different not just between the traditional and modern societies but also among the modern ones as well. For example, France (86) and Germany (65) are higher in UA than those of Great Britain (35) and the United States (46). Pakistan (70) was higher than Iran (59). Greece scored the highest (112) and Singapore the lowest in the survey mentioned by Hofstede.[23] Afghanistan was not a participant in the survey. However, had it been, its score would have been high and closer to those of Pakistan and Iran.

Tolerance, the first criterion of measuring level of uncertainty avoidance, involves stress and anxiety. Stress has different sources. One is personal. Some individuals have type A personalities while others are type B. The former experiences more stress than the latter. The workplace is another source of stress and anxiety. For example, non-government jobs are more stressful than government jobs in Afghanistan. In the former case, promotions and job maintenance are usually based on performance; whereas in the latter, other factors such as connections, nepotism, and obedience are usually more important than performance. Government jobs in Afghanistan can be stressful only if the supervisor is authoritarian and strict.

The workplace is not the only place where stress plays a role. In the family and other social organizations, too, stress and anxiety exist. For instance, in an Afghan family, if the father is a type A personality, he is usually more authoritarian and gets angry at his wife and children, making life very difficult for the family members. If, on the other hand, the head of the family is of the type B personality, he is less authoritarian and the environment relatively less stressful. Finally, society at large can also be the source of stress. Countries such as Afghanistan allow their members to express their emotions in public whereas others, such as the United States, do not. Americans are taught to manage their anger. This explains why Afghans get mad and yell in public and in private more than the Americans, the British and other Western societies. This may seem uncivilized, but it is good for the heart if individuals can express their emotions and frustrations and get it off their chest. There have not been any studies of Afghan Americans, but according to some studies, Japanese Americans suffer more from heart disease than the Japanese because the Japanese society allows its members to express their emotions. How a society handles uncertainty is determined by its cultural heritage and collectively held values that are transferred from generation to generation and strengthened in the family, schools, and other organizations in society.

Methods

According to Hofstede, societies use three methods to minimize uncertainty and fear: technology, law, and religion. "Technology includes all human artifacts; law, rules that guide social behavior; religion, all revealed knowledge of the unknown . . . Technology has helped us to defend ourselves against uncertainties caused by nature; law, to defend against uncertainties in the behavior of others; religion, to accept the uncertainties we cannot defend ourselves against."[24] These methods are similar to what some anthropologists call "games" traditional cultures play: games of physical skill involving mastery of the self and the environment, games of strategy involving mastery of the social system, and games of chance involving mastery of the supernatural[25].

All societies employ these three mechanisms to reduce fear and ambiguity and bring about normalcy to their lives, not just in the workplace but in society at large. How they differ is in the frequency and type of method used. For example, modern technological societies usually make more use of technology and rules, whereas traditional and developing societies such as Afghanistan usually use more religion to cope with uncertainty and bring normalcy to life.

Technology—artifacts, objects, gadgets, and other things—created by humans to serve a purpose in life, is an important defining characteristic of modern societies and is used to lessen uncertainty even though it has its drawbacks. Despite its side effects, technology has made life a lot less stressful for humans. The use of surveillance cameras in banks and stores, for example, serves the purpose of preventing thefts and robberies. They may or may not achieve their purpose, but they give the bankers and shop owners a degree of peace of mind and thereby reduce uncertainty.

These are examples of how cultures deal with fear from other men. Technology can also be employed to cope with nature and the supernatural. Equipment used for controlling heat and cold and forecasting weather conditions, for instance, reduce fear and ambiguity caused by nature. Here again, taking the necessary precautions provides some normalcy and peace of mind to humans. Technology can also lessen fear of the supernatural. Loudspeakers in mosques in the Islamic world, for example, help Muslims not to miss prayer times, thus keeping God happy and preventing them punishment on the Day of Judgment. The use of clocks and watches serve the same purpose.

The second method, laws, also reduces uncertainty and fear. Laws can be criminal or civil, secular or religious, good or bad, formal or informal, written or unwritten including rules and rituals. According to Hofstede, rules are semi-rational while rituals are non-rational.[26] Not all rules, however, are related to the workplace. Some rules are necessary for social relations and cohesiveness in society. Coming to a party at the designated hour, for example, is a social rule whereas coming to work at a fixed time is a work-related rule. Memos and meetings are examples of rituals in the workplace, while shaking hands is a social ritual.

The purpose of rules is to create predictable behavior. To ensure that employees work from 8:00 in the morning until 5:00 in the afternoon, to see that drivers stop at a red traffic light or to make people pay their taxes and so on, rules are necessary. Prediction in turn reduces uncertainty and ambiguity and gives life the appearance of normalcy. Organizations use rules and regulations to reduce internal uncertainty. In fact, they are the essence of a bureaucracy.

Finally, religion, the third method of reducing uncertainty, also, plays a role in reducing fear and ambiguity not just in the workplace but also in the family and society in general. When I was in Saudi Arabia, the dean of our college led the prayers. All professors had to pray regardless of whether they were practicing Muslims or not. Not doing so would have jeopardized their promotions and even their jobs, especially those of the non-Saudis. Thus, the purpose of praying at the college was to reduce fear and uncertainty on the part of the faculty and staff. The same is true in Afghan schools, especially nowadays when religiosity is on the rise. In the family, too, religion is important in reducing uncertainty. In many Afghan families, one has to begin eating by reciting the Arabic utterance, "in the name of God" to avoid the anger of parents. Religion, as it will be made clear, dominates Afghan society as it is used to reduce fear not just from God but also from other men and nature. Religion reinforces differences in uncertainty avoidance in societies.

Ideologies, according to Hofstede, are very similar to religion in that they are secular religions. In the more uncertainty-avoiding societies, ideologies are more likely to be dogmatic and intolerant of opposing ones. "In general, we can expect that problems more often will be looked at ideologically in higher UAI countries and pragmatically in lower UAI."[27]

Consequences of Uncertainty Avoidance

Uncertainty avoidance is associated with political systems, dependence on experts, seniority, and theory versus practice in society, which are all consequences of cultural norms, according to Hofstede.[28]

The Political System. The more uncertainty-avoiding cultures such as Afghanistan are associated with unbalanced government and the less avoiding ones such as the United States with balanced government. This aspect of the political system falls under power distance discussed in the previous chapter. But the political system also relates to uncertainty avoidance. Citizen competence, in less uncertainty-avoiding societies such as the United States, means that citizens feel free to protest decisions in the workplace and those made at the local and national levels. They have a role to play in changing the political system through their participation in local and national politics. In more uncertainty-avoiding societies such as Afghanistan, on the other hand, there is citizen incompetence: the citizens feel they cannot protest decisions, and they are powerless in their ability to change the system in the workplace and the society at large.

Dependence on Expert. In the more uncertainty-avoiding cultures, there is more emphasis on expert knowledge than in less uncertainty-avoiding ones. Some tasks such as managerial ones are performed by laymen in the latter societies but not in the former. Traditionally, in Afghanistan, almost all the ministers and other administrators have been experts rather than, managers. The minister of health, for example, has always been a medical doctor and that of mines a mining engineer or geologist, and so on. In low UA societies such as the United States, on the other hand, managers are not usually experts in what they are managing, but they are experts in managing. For example, the secretary of defense in the United States is not a soldier, a marine, or a seaman. Instead, he is a civilian and a manager.

Seniority. In more uncertainty-avoiding societies, there is a generation gap. Older people tend to wait longer before allowing the young to take responsibilities in their hands. As it was pointed out in the previous chapter, old age is a source of power in Afghanistan. Afghans trust older people in their judgment and decision making. They approve of their behavior while more often disapprove of actions taken by younger people. This is especially the case with the ruler or the head of state. Usually, a ruler less than, at least, fifty years of age is not respected by the citizens. In Afghanistan, there is an age difference between the leaders and followers. In short, there is gerontocracy or rule of the old in the country.

Theory versus Practice. UA norms have a deep effect on intellectual activity. Less uncertainty-avoiding societies are associated with empirical research, whereas high ones are theoretical and ideological. Hence, most Nobel Prize winners come from low UAI countries such as the United States. Theories in the social sciences are associated with high UAI such as Germany and France, which are known for their philosophers and theoreticians.

Countries on the more uncertainty avoidance side tend to explain problems theoretically or ideologically as opposed to pragmatically or practically, regardless of whether the problems are social, political, economic, or otherwise. In academia, in these cultures, there is more emphasis on theoretical research than experimentation and empirical work. In Afghanistan, at the Faculty of Agriculture, Kabul University, for example, students study mainly theoretical subjects while paying very little attention to the application of this knowledge to the improvement of grapes, for example, or other crops in Afghanistan. The same is true about other faculties at the universities and institutions of higher education in Afghanistan. This is in big contrast to the community colleges in the United States, which serve the needs of specific communities.

Social problems are also explained on religious or ideological basis. For example, some Islamists believe imitating the West leads to the destruction of Islam and the Afghan way of life, without making any distinctions in practical terms between Western technological know-how, a necessity for developing societies such as Afghanistan, and Western social values such as dating, which would be damaging to the social fabric of Afghan society.

How Afghans Cope with Uncertainty

As any other society, Afghans make use of technology, law, and religion. But for reasons to be made clear shortly, Afghans depend heavily on religion more than technology and law to cope with fear, ambiguity, and uncertainty.

Technology. There is very little modern technology available to most Afghans, especially those living in the countryside and provinces. The rich and powerful (perhaps less than 1 percent) have access to almost all the modern conveniences: electricity twenty-four hours a day, running water, air conditioning and heating, satellite television, kitchen appliances, telephone, computers and other electronic devices, the best furniture, washers and driers, and so forth. But for most Afghans, life is very primitive, and even clean drinking water is not available for many Afghans in the capital Kabul and other cities.

To illustrate, let us compare how a housewife prepares a meal here in America and in Afghanistan. Here, in Modesto, California, my wife thinks of lunch no more than an hour before noon. Processed food, kitchen appliances, running water, cooking utensils, and other gadgets make it possible to prepare a hot meal of rice, chicken, and spinach in less than an hour. The chicken is chopped up, the spinach washed, and the rice is clean. All she has to do is cook the ingredients on a stove in three different pots simultaneously.

Preparing such a meal in Kabul, Afghanistan, on the other hand, is a lot harder and is time-consuming even for a family of above average income. My brother's wife has to think about lunch as soon as she is done with breakfast. To prepare the same meal, she has to clean, cut, and wash the chicken out in the yard (in the countryside, the chicken has to be slaughtered by a male, and then it has to be plucked of feathers and chopped up, which could take at least an hour). Unlike the rice imported to the United Sates, the rice sold in Afghanistan is not clean.[29] She needs to clean the rice of small pieces of stone and other foreign elements, taking at least thirty to forty-five minutes. Then, she has to wash the spinach to separate the mud, roots, and other undesirable elements in the kitchen located in the compound corner because there is no running water. The water for washing, too, must be obtained from the well with a manual pump. This process takes at least another thirty to forty minutes. Then, she has to cook these ingredients one at a time on a kerosene stove since power is not available 24-7 for most residents of Kabul. She must cook the rice last, or it to would not be warm at the time of serving. Some families, even in Kabul, the capital, use firewood to cook food, as kerosene is more expensive. Cooking the chicken, spinach, and rice takes at least thirty minutes each. Thus, preparing a hot meal takes all morning in Afghanistan.

Life in the countryside and villages is a lot worse, and people do not have the basic services. People still mostly use the technology of the Middles Ages. Farming, cooking, heating, washing clothes, housing construction, treating the sick, and so on involve very little, if any, modern medicine and technology.

Traveling inside the cities and out to the provinces is also hard and time-consuming. Public transportation is insufficient and not usually on schedule. Afghans in urban areas depend on public and private buses and vans to move around. Since such transportation is not reliable, most people depend on bicycles to get from place to place. In the countryside, it is mostly bicycles and donkeys.

With the exception of some major districts, in urban areas including Kabul, streets and houses have no names, making it hard to locate residential and commercial places. Unless you have been to the place before, it takes hours to find, thus making it necessary to ask several times where the destination is.

Until recently, even in Kabul, there were no public restrooms and almost all restaurants do not have restrooms, forcing people to relieve themselves in mosque restrooms, alleys and/or even in the Kabul Riverbed in the summer when there is very little or no water.

Since there is no sewage system, even in the capital, a very small number of houses have cesspools. The rest have their "restrooms" (*baitulkhalaa* or *badaraft*) inside the compounds with an outlet inside the compound or on the streets and alleys. The odor in these alleys is terrible, even for Afghans who are used to it. Highways have no "rest areas," and neither are there signs indicating speed, distance, or other pertinent information for travelers.

Usually, there is no mail delivery to private homes. One has to have a post office box or have his or her mail delivered to a shop. The mailboxes are usually for mail from the provinces or abroad. Local communication is usually face-to-face or by phone. Written correspondence is hand delivered. For example, wedding and other invitation cards are hand carried to various homes.

In communications technology, too, Afghans are deprived of the very basics. Most Afghan households have access only to battery-operated radios due to the problem of electricity, which is available only in major cities and towns and only for certain hours a day. This includes the capital Kabul, too. This is why even in major cities and towns people have to have battery-operated radios instead of plug-in ones in order to listen to the news, music, and other programs. Those who can afford it have generators to produce electricity but most do not. Television sets are too expensive for the average Afghan family; and even for those who can afford them, their use is limited due to the absence of power 24-7. Afghans have the same problem with personal computers: their price and lack of electricity on a regular basis make them beyond the reach of most Afghans. Thus, lack of electricity deprives the majority of Afghans of the basic technologies.[30] Telephones, another vital communication gadget, are not available to most Afghans either. The owners of cell phones probably make only 1 percent of the population of Afghanistan. In emergencies, the majority of Afghans cannot call a doctor or a hospital for example. They have to take the patient there in a taxi, a bicycle, or a donkey. In the countryside, donkeys and bicycles are the primary means of transportation. That is why donkeys are referred by some outside observers as the "jeeps of Afghanistan."

Air conditioning, still another necessity in the modern world, does not exist in Afghanistan. When I told my relatives in Kabul during my visit two years ago that in America, we have in our home what is called a thermostat and can set it to get heat or cold air, they were shocked. They hadn't heard of air-conditioning. Afghans use fans and heaters whose usage is limited, due to lack of power on a regular basis. In the absence of electricity, people use charcoal and firewood for heating and cooking. Heat in the summer and cold in the winter can be very severe in certain regions. There is a joke about Jelalabad, east of Kabul. Afghans say that the city is so hot that only two types of creatures live there in the summer: dogs and government employees. Thus, there is very little technology available to Afghans to defend themselves against nature.

Just as there is not much technology to reduce fear of nature, there is very little use of technology to lessen fear of other humans. Instead of theft alarms, some Afghans use watchdogs;[31] but for most people, door locks and high walls are the only defense against other men, even in

Kabul, the capital. There is no 911 to call the police. When and if the police arrive, it is usually too late. That is why in Afghanistan, you have to depend on yourself against an attacker instead of the law enforcers. Unfortunately, weapons are the only technology of which is plentiful in the country nowadays. Prior to the invasion of the Soviet Union and the subsequent civil war, Afghans used sticks and knives if fights broke out in the neighborhood. Now, however, they use automatic rifles and even RPGs (rocket-propelled grenades).

Law

The purpose of law is to protect one man from another man and reduce fear and uncertainty. There are two major types of rules: the rule of law and the rule of the ruler. In the rule of law, common in Western democracies, all citizens are equal before the law; no one is above the law. In less uncertainty-avoiding societies such as the United States, even the president can be impeached as well as the vice president, members of the cabinet, congressmen, governors, mayors, and other individuals in public or private life.

But in the rule of the ruler—widespread in the third world and more uncertainty-avoiding societies such as Afghanistan—the rulers and those in positions of power make and manipulate laws to control the citizens and stay in power. That is why presidents are rarely impeached, and other top government officials and others in positions of power and influence are rarely prosecuted for wrongdoing. They are above the law; only the weak and powerless are supposed to abide by the laws. Instead of government of the people, by the people, and for the people, it is government of the ruler, for the ruler, and by the ruler. In fact, these days it is rather government of the *rulers* as there are multiple centers of power in the country. At one time, there was a very powerful minister named Popal, connected to the royal family. The joke was that, in Afghanistan, it was government of the Popal, for the Popal, and by the Popal, rather than government of the people, by the people, and for the people.

There are laws, rules, and regulations, but they are patchy and unevenly enforced. Consequently, the average citizen does not trust the police and other law enforcement agencies. Corruption is rampant in courts and other departments of the government bureaucracy. Without money, connections, or both, it is difficult, if not impossible, to get anything done whether it is a lawsuit, obtaining a passport, a driver's license, getting a job, or anything else.

If the neighbor's son beats up your son and he happens to be the son of the chief of police, a minister or any other person of power and influence, there is nothing you can do. Without 911 to call, even if and when the police arrive, he is not arrested. Even if arrested, he will be released. Getting into a fight with the neighbor is just not a good option, either unless you are rich or have connections. The simple reason is that you will be the loser and the culprit the winner. That is why in such situations, Afghans swallow their pride and wait for the right time and place to settle the score with the neighbors, or they pray that God would punish him. Thus, in Afghanistan, for the majority of the population, the law is not an effective method for avoiding fear of other human beings. Nowadays, rule of the gun is added to the rule of the ruler, making life even more difficult for the average Afghan.

In the absence of the rule of law to protect Afghans from other human beings and very little technology to defend themselves against nature, one would think that life must be very stressful for Afghans. On the contrary, it is not.

Afghans cope. It is said that Afghans are known for their endurance of hardship. There are several explanations. One is that, compared to modern living, primitive life is much less complicated and a lot less stressful. Prior to my immigrating to the United States in 1980, I had traveled to America several times back and forth. I have lived both here and in Afghanistan. In the United States, life is much more stressful than in Afghanistan. In America, I need to worry about so many things: from parking my car to insurance, to paying my bills on time, to watching my diet. Living in Afghanistan was rather simple because I did not have to worry about so many things.

Another reason why life is not so stressful for Afghans might be ignorance or lack of education. If you have not lived in a democratic environment, you don't miss freedom, and it does not bother you when you don't have it. If you have never tasted ice cream, it does not bother you when it is not available. The same is true about air conditioning and other modern conveniences. One has to experience something to miss it. However, experience, of course, does not have to be direct. One can indirectly learn about how other people live, either through reading or listening to the radio or watching movies. But doing so requires literacy and access to reading materials, radio and television, as well as movies. Most Afghans (perhaps 80 percent) lack functional literacy and, as it has already been pointed out, also lack of electricity. They also lack the money to buy television sets and personal computers. And the scarcity of movie theaters make such experiences hard to come by. Thus, low citizen competency keeps Afghans ignorant about modern living. This low competence, in turn, tends to make life less stressful for them.

However, simple living and low citizen competency alone cannot explain why Afghans endure so much stress, injustice, hardship, and other sufferings. Religion, the third method of uncertainty avoidance, may be the primary reason behind it. As it will be made clear, religion plays a pivotal role in reducing fear not just from the supernatural but also from nature and other human beings.

Religion

Mainstream Islam, proxy Islam, Sufism, and cultural traditions form attitudes and beliefs about life and death in Afghan society. At the core of these are three fundamental beliefs that reduce the uncertainties of daily life in the country. It is worth noting that it is not only the ordinary Afghans who adhere to these beliefs; some well-educated Afghans who hold degrees in engineering and medicine and other natural science fields also adhere to such beliefs.

One is the belief that life here on earth is temporary and it is life after death that matters and is permanent. This world is a "testing stage" for God's subjects. How one lives in this world determines how one lives in the next world. Those who stay in the path of God will be rewarded, but deviators will be punished, though all Muslims eventually go to paradise. Emphasis on spiritualism rather than materialism in life is an important tenet of Sufism, i.e., Islamic mysticism. The more one suffers hardship the more likely one is to reach God, according to Sufism.

There is an interesting story related to the temporary nature of life. It is said that a king, perhaps Sultan Mahmood Ghaznawi, who ruled about one thousand years ago, asked his vizier to make something for him so upon seeing it he would become happy if he was sad and vice versa. The vizier ordered that a ring be made for the king, and on the ring it should be scribed the Dari sentence, "*Ein ham maygozarad*" (This, too, is temporary.) Every time the king felt happy, looking at the ring made him sad because the happiness would not last long. Similarly, when he felt sad, looking at the ring made him happy because he knew it would not last long. The relevance of this belief in uncertainty avoidance is that this belief provides Afghans, most of whom live in poverty, a psychological relief from adversity and hardship due to its temporary nature.

Another fundamental belief is that nothing in the world happens without the will of God, not even the movement of tree leaves. This implies that God is the source of both good (*khair*) and evil (*shar*). Therefore, one has to accept the ups and downs of life with open arms since God knows best. This raises the issue of free will (*ekhteyaar*) versus predestination (*jabr*). If God is responsible for what happens, then what is man's responsibility? This philosophical issue has been debated for centuries among the ulema (Islamic scholars) in the Islamic world as well as philosophers in the West. The point is that the average Afghan accepts divine will. There is some logic to this view because most Afghans are not in control of their lives, making fatalism the best defense against fear and uncertainty.

Unlike the United States and other less uncertainty-avoiding societies, **life** in Afghanistan is not a matter of **choice** but a matter of **chance** because people are not usually in control of their lives. For the same reason, planning, especially long-term, is not part of the Afghan culture. Furthermore, due to the dominance of religion, there is a gap between action and words or desired and desirable values in Afghan society. It is not surprising why Afghans and other Muslims use the Arabic phrase *Insha'Allah* ("God willing") when it comes to events or actions taking place in the future. The reason is that they are not certain about the will of God. Sometimes this phrase is used as an excuse for not doing what has been promised. Fatalism, of course, does not mean Afghans just sit and let events take over. What it means is that they do not want to take the blame if something goes wrong. Not feeling guilt in turn provides relief and peace of mind.

Finally, there is the belief that God is just. God punishes the oppressor in this world and the next. Thus, the neighbor whose son was cruel will somehow be punished by God because He is just and fair. The same happens to rulers, governors, chiefs of police, and others who are unjust and commit crimes against the subjects of God. It is due to these fundamental beliefs and traditions in the form of rituals that Afghans can cope with the fears and uncertainties of life with regard to nature, man, and the supernatural.

Religion can also help in coping with nature. Rain, for example, is said to be the mercy of God, but flooding is His anger. Natural calamities such as flooding, drought and earthquakes are signs of God's anger. They are to warn His subjects not to deviate from the path of God. The average believer repents and asks for the mercy of God, so such calamities are not repeated. In case of a drought, for example, they even give charity (*khairaat*) in the form of cooking food for the poor. In their daily prayers, too, they ask God to cure a disease. But they may also go to a mullah for an emulate, or a holy man for his blessing or to a shrine. Many Afghans, especially the uneducated, believe in miracles of holy shrines and saints. For example, every year hundreds of thousands go to Mazar-e Sharif to attend the ceremony of *Janda* at the shrine believed to be the tomb of Ali, the fourth caliph and son-in-law of the Prophet, to ask for miracles. It is said that some blind people have regained their sight at the shrine. Others have said their wishes have come true because of miracles of the shrine. During the rest of the year, tens of thousands of people, especially the Shi'is, followers of Ali, visit various shrines. Muslims, except the Saudi Wahabis, believe in shrines, saints and holy men. That is why every village, town, and city has such shrines that men and women go to for a variety of purposes. Some go to cure their sickness others to make their wishes come true, and still others visit them because it is spiritual.

Before starting work, they pray so it will be easy and successful. This also explains why Afghans use *Insha'Allah* or "God willing" about work to be done in a future time. Before traveling long distances, a copy of the Qur'an is held above the head of the traveler to pass under to prevent accidents or other mishaps on the way.

Religion is employed to reduce fear of other people in a variety of ways. One is to deal with local and foreign opponents. On the local level, religious sects have been used to fighting opponents. For example, the Pashtun Taliban attacked the Hazaras for being Shi'i. To the orthodox Sunni Pashtuns, Hazara Shi'is are apostates. Islamists also declare jihad against their local opponents for imitating or associating too closely with the West.

God will punish oppressors and evildoers. Therefore, one has to be patient about them. If one is in love and wants to marry her but the girl's parents refuse the engagement, one goes to the mullah for an emulate or to a shrine for a miracle, hoping the girl's parents will change their minds about marrying their daughter to this boy.

The beliefs and practices discussed above are indicative of the fact that God is both a source of comfort and of fear. In a recent Afghan-made CD, the owners state at the very beginning: "Whoever copies this CD without permission should confront the anger of God." This is probably more effective than an "FBI Warning" in North America and other Western nations to prevent copying. To avoid the anger of God and punishment both in this life and the one after, Afghans must do the required in worshipping God (*ebaadaat*) and their dealings with other individuals (*muaamelaat*). The worship includes the five pillars of

Islam: declaring the faith (*kaleema*), praying five times a day (*namaz*), fasting (*rowza*), almsgiving (*zakaat*) and pilgrimage to Mecca (*hajj*). Muaamelat includes business and trade, marriage, and other things that involve dealing with other individuals. One has to do well in both *ebaadaat* and *muaamelaat* to avoid God's anger.

Uncertainty Avoidance in the Workplace

Government jobs are less stressful than the private ones because there is not much supervision and performance evaluation in the former. Generally speaking, in the Afghan workplace, planning, especially long-term planning, is almost nonexistent; individual competition is disliked and least preferred, and coworkers are described very unfavorably.

As a supervisor of the Afghans, the Westerner should work more on goals and strategies, performance criteria, competition, teamwork, and work ethic. Since Afghan employees are usually deprived of participating in decision making, it would be good to get them involved through group and individual discussions and consultations. Afghans tend not to complain or challenge the supervisor openly. Therefore, it is important to consult the employees in private and on an individual basis and encourage them to express their views. Older employees need to be respected and their views sought. In assigning committees, putting younger employees in charge is not productive. If the older employee is not very competent, it is better to assign a more competent person as his assistant. Additionally, Afghans are not used to frequent meetings, writing memos and reports, or meeting deadlines. Once, however, a purpose and format is made clear, they will participate in such rituals in the workplace. Also, Afghans need to be allowed to pray at work and attend funerals of close relatives during work hours, as these religious rituals are very sensitive and important in the culture. Still, and more importantly, rules and regulations must be explained at the very beginning, and they must be strictly enforced without exceptions, and violators need to be reprimanded. As members of a society on the high side of uncertainty avoidance, Afghans prefer written rules. Finally, a Westerner needs to be aware of the fact that Afghans are less risk taking, have strong egos, and aggressive behavior of self and others is accepted. It must be kept in mind that Afghans are very proud people. Therefore, they should be treated with respect and their dignity kept intact.

Conclusions

Afghanistan is among the more uncertainty-avoiding countries and shares some of their characteristics. Afghan cultural norms influence the political system, age gap, legislation, theoretical/ideological approaches to problems and dependence on experts. Of the three methods of coping with uncertainty, Afghans make heavier use of religion than technology and laws; they use the three fundamentals of Islam and tradition: the will and justice of God and the temporary nature of life on earth. Afghans use religion to deal not just with the supernatural but also with nature and society. This is due to the facts that there is very little modern technology and laws are patchy and unevenly enforced. Uncertainty avoidance in Afghanistan has implications for the Westerner to keep in mind in order to work effectively with Afghans.

Afghans, unlike Americans, fear the government. Afghans fear lack of food (quantity), whereas Americans worry about eating less and avoiding unhealthy food (quality). Afghans eat to live while Americans live to eat. Afghans worry more about basic human needs; Americans worry more about individual freedoms and rights. Afghans worry about not just immediate family but also extended family. If Afghans pay more attention to the present rather than the future, Americans pay attention not just to the present but also the future (planning and saving money). Afghans usually accept their parents' decisions and stay with them until they pass away while Americans often do not. Finally, Afghans worry about their children even after they are grown up, but Americans often do not. Some of these cultural differences involve collectivism versus individualism, the third dimension of culture and the subject of the next chapter.

Food for Thought

(1) Why is it that Afghans usually don't stay in line and await their turn whether it is getting on a bus or obtaining tickets at a movie theater?

(2) In Shi'i Islam, there is *taqiya* according to which one can hide his or her true religion if being truthful is dangerous. Why is *taqiya* important for the Shi's in Afghanistan?

(3) In Afghanistan, instead of saying someone passed away they say he or she became "martyred" or "fulfilled the will of God." Why?

(4) Is it true that some Afghans are more tolerant of misfortune and hardship according to their degree of religiosity? Why?

(5) Why are Afghans punctual when it comes to movie theaters, doctors, or employment appointments but not when going to parties, weddings, and other social gatherings?

(6) Why is it that authority of the rule does not carry much weight in Afghanistan?

(7) Afghan youth today are much more religious than during the period prior to the Civil War. What are the reasons for this change?

(8) Unlike Sunnism, Shi'ism places more emphasis on personal responsibility in coping with life while accepting the will of God. Why?

(9) Do Afghans live to work or work to live? Why? How about Americans?

(10) What should you do to handle your cook or guards to prevent problems and surprises, especially when they have not worked for foreigners before?

(11) What are the consequences of uncertainty avoidance in Afghan schools, employment, the family, and investment in the country Why?

(12) Since Afghans have less motivation for achievement compared to Americans, what are the consequences of this cultural trait in education, the workplace, and business? Explain.

(13) Afghans prefer specialist careers to managerial ones. What are the consequences of this cultural trait in the labor force?

(14) Is time gold in Afghanistan? Why, or why not?

(15) Why is it that Afghans are usually hesitant to try new food?

(16) Why do Afghans reciprocate gifts and favors and take this seriously?

(17) Why do Afghans usually cook more than they can eat at one setting?

Author seated third from the right, wearing a tie. Kabul 2003.

CHAPTER 3

Individualism and Collectivism

Blood is thicker than water.
—Hazaragi proverb

Introduction

When the Taliban came to power in Afghanistan, they destroyed the Buddha statues in Bamiyan Province, resulting in international outrage and condemnation of the movement. The Afghans, too, condemned the Taliban action inside and outside of the country. Most of the Pashtuns, however, refrained from public condemnation of the Taliban. So I asked a well-educated Pashtun in the United States, who shall remain anonymous, why the Pashtuns had been silent on this issue. He said that condemnation of the Taliban would benefit the late Ahmad Shah Massoud, who was at the time the only opposition to the Taliban in the country. I replied that the Pakistan government would benefit from not condemning the Taliban. I also added that it was better for an Afghan, Massoud, to benefit than a foreign country. He kept silent. This is an example of ethnic loyalty, which calls for weakening and undermining rivals, even if it is not in the national interest. Generally speaking, members of one ethnic group do not criticize leaders of their own group no matter how bad they may be. Ahmad Shah Massoud was a Tajik and the Taliban mostly Pashtuns.

Group loyalty is related to the third dimension of culture: individualism versus collectivism.

According to Hofstede,[32] individualism (IND) versus collectivism involves the relationship of individuals to groups or collectivity. It is negatively related to power distance; high PD societies are less individualistic, whereas low PD societies are more individualistic. In collectivistic cultures such as Afghanistan, individuals are at the service of the collectivity, namely, the family, ethnic groups or other collectivities. Important decisions in life such as marriage, education, occupation, ideology, travel, and others are made by the family rather than by the individuals; deviations on the part of the individuals on such issues can have negative consequences. Group solidarity is an important characteristic of collectivist societies. Individuals rely more on the family and other collectivity for their protection and advancement than on the government. The collectivity is also responsible for the improper behavior of individuals in society. Thus, it is a common practice in Afghanistan to make the family, clan, tribe, or the entire community responsible for the behavior of its members. For instance, if someone in a family commits a crime and runs away, the police arrest his father or his brother and force him to find the suspect.

Individualism or collectivism affects family and society at large. Extended families are associated with collectivism, whereas nuclear families are individualistic. This change is due to modernism and industrialization. In other words, the more modern a society, the less complex the family. How modernization affects man's attitudes is best summarized in the following:

Modern . . . man is open to new experiences; relatively independent of parental authority; concerned with time, planning, willing to defer

gratification; he feels man can be the master over nature, and that he controls the reinforcements he receives from his environment; he believes in determinism and science; he has a wide, cosmopolitan perspective, he uses broad ingroups; he competes with standards of excellence, and he is optimistic about controlling his environment. Traditional man has narrow ingroups, looks at the world with suspicion, believes that good is limited, and one obtains a share of it by chance or pleasing the gods; he identifies with his parents and receives direction from them; he considers planning a waste of time, and does not defer gratification; he feels at the mercy of obscure environmental factors, and is prone to mysticism; he sees interpersonal relations as an end, rarely as means to an end; he does not believe that he can control his environment but rather sees himself under the influence of external, mystical powers.[33]

Collectivism is negatively related to economic development. Collectivist cultures are lees economically developed than individualistic cultures. This is because "technologies developed in Western individualistic settings more or less presuppose an individualist mentality in entrepreneurs, managers and workers which are part of modernity."[34]

Collectivism or individualism has its origins and consequences.[35] On the origins of low individualistic societies such as Afghanistan, aside from low economic development, in these cultures there is less social mobility and a weak development of the middle class; survival is less dependent on individual initiative. Collectivistic societies utilize more traditional agriculture, less modern industry, less urbanization. Other characteristics are extended family or tribal structure, more children per nuclear family, traditional educational systems for a minority of the population, collectivist thinking and action (religion and ideology), and smaller organization (government).

As to the consequences of collectivist cultures, the following traits, mentioned by Hostede, are relevant to the Afghan culture: less occupational mobility, more income inequality, less press freedom, more repression potential, more collective conversion, and policies and practices, which vary according to relations involving family, tribe, region, ideology, and so on.

In collective societies such as Afghanistan, people from childhood onward are integrated into strong cohesive ingroups, which protect them in exchange for their unquestioning loyalty. These ingroups in the Afghanistan are best explained under the rubric of Afghan nationalism.

Afghan Nationalism

To understand Afghan nationalism, it is important to briefly discuss the individual rights and privacy common in individualistic societies of the West, which is almost nonexistent in societies such as Afghanistan. For example, one's age, clothing, marital status, income, and so on are personal matters in America but not in Afghanistan. That is why it is normal for Afghans to ask such questions when meeting Americans: "Why aren't you married?" "How much is your salary?" "How old is your wife?" "Why don't you live with your parents?" The same is true about physical space, which does not exist. In individualistic societies such as the United States, an individual has the privacy of space that must be maintained. In Afghanistan, there is no such privacy: two men can sit or stand next to each other without any space in between and even touch each other. In America, holding hands between a man and a woman in public is a private matter but not in Afghanistan.

Lack of individual rights, however, is much more serious. The word for *citizen* in Pashto, Dari, and other languages spoken in Afghanistan is an Arabic word *taba'a* meaning "subject." Even the new constitution of Afghanistan uses this Arabic word when referring to its citizens. The traditional national identity card, *tazkera-ye tabi'iyat* (literally biography of *taba'a*, a subject) specifies one's name, father's name, date and place of birth, ethnicity, gender, religion, special physical features, military service, and so on. In English, the word *citizen* is defined as "an individual with rights and privileges," whereas the word *taba'a* means "subject" or "one who obeys" with no mention of rights.

In the absence of the rule of law and protection of rights in collectivist societies such as Afghanistan, people identify with and depend on their family, ethnic group, and other collectivity for protection and advancement. That is why residents of Afghanistan are first Pashtuns, Tajiks, Hazaras, Uzbeks, and so on and only secondly, Afghans. Family, ethnicity, and other group interests usually have priority to the national interests. This raises the issue of nationalism, which, as it will shortly be made clear, is not the same in the East as in the West.

In the West, the word *nationalism* means "loyalty and devotion to a nation" [Since nationalism in the West has a negative connotation due to German nationalism and World War II, the word "patriotism" is more common.] Besides, in societies on the high side of uncertainty avoidance such as Afghanistan, people are more "nationalistic" than those on the low side of uncertainty avoidance such as the United States]. That is why in Afghanistan and other countries of the East, *nationalism* usually means loyalty and devotion to one's family, ethnicity (including race and language), and so on. It would not be an exaggeration to say that "Afghanistan" consists of several nations or "ISTANs": "Pashtunistan" (Pashtuns), "Tajikistan" (Tajiks), "Hazaristan" (Hazaras), "Uzbekistan" (Uzbeks), "Turkmenistan," (Turkmens) and so on. Loyalty and devotion is first and foremost to these STANs and other collectivities. Hamid Karzai was probably the first Afghan who, in 2001, said he was first an Afghan and then a Pashtun.

To shed more light on Afghan nationalism, let us briefly examine the words *Afghanistan* and *Afghan*. The word *afghanistan* literally means "land of the afghans." There are different theories on how this country got its name. One is that the Persians (now Iranians) referred to the tribes in its eastern region as *afaghena* (Arabic for the plural of the word *afghan*). Within Afghanistan, too, the Tajiks and other minority ethnic groups call the Pashtuns *Afghans*, not Pashtuns. Some non-Pashtuns even refer to the Pashto language as *afghani*, (Afghan) instead of Pahto. However, with the exception of Afghan Millat (Afghan Nation), a Pashtun nationalist political party, the Pashtuns call themselves "Pashtana or Pakhtana" or Pashtuns, not "Afghans." Ahmad Shah Durrani, who founded modern Afghanistan, could have called it "Pahtunistan" rather than "Afghanistan." Almost all the rulers of modern Afghanistan since 1747 have been Pashtuns, including the current president, Hamid Karzai.

Some non-Pashtuns, who make up the other 60 percent of the population, object to the name *Afghanistan* because to them it means "land of the Pashtuns." They maintain that *Afghanistan* is a "misnomer" and the country should be called "Khurasan"[36] instead. Some even go one step further and say that until the name of the country changes to "Khurasan," a person from Afghanistan should be called an "Afghanistani" rather than an "Afghan." Reacting to a recent attempt on the part of the government of Afghanistan to issue identification cards to Afghan citizens on a trial basis, the Society of Ethnic Turks in Afghanistan has expressed its violent opposition to calling all the ethnic groups "Afghan." It states that "the word 'afghan' is synonymous to the word 'Pashtun.' Identifying all the ethnic groups in the country with this word is not only sensitive and provocative but also a violation of human rights and civil, political, and international convention. Nowhere in the world is the name of one ethnic group imposed on the others . . . For example, in Uzbekistan, Russian, Tajik, Turkmen, Qazaq (Kazakh), Armenian, Kyrgyz, Jewish, Arab and other citizens of the country are not called Uzbek in their ID cards or passports. Rather, they are all identified with the name of their country, Uzbekistan. This procedure is followed throughout Asia, Europe, American and even African countries."[37] In other words, to the Turkic ethnic groups of Afghanistan, their nationality should be "Afghanistan" rather than "Afghan." Thus, not all Afghans are in agreement even in the name of the country.

To illustrate further that Afghanistan is a nation of nations, the analogy of a Chinese box is probably appropriate. Within the big box of Afghanistan, there are smaller boxes of decreasing size. The Pashtuns (40 percent) make up the second "box," followed by the Tajiks (27 percent), Hazaras (18 percent), Uzbeks (9 percent), and so on.[38] McChesney provides an excellent description of this Chinese box when he says, "Afghanistan's international borders were drawn during the last decades of the nineteenth century, at the initiative of and generally in accordance with the concern of British for the security of its colonial possessions in South Asia. A nation of nations was thereby created, a grab bag of ethnic groups with little in common historically, speaking . . . distinct languages . . . and with identities so local that in the middle of the twentieth century people in Kandahar thought of Kabulis just as foreign as someone from Germany or China." He goes on and correctly adds that "within the territory itself, history produces little evidence of a national sense of belonging or loyalty extending much beyond family, clan, and village. Instances of apparent unity in the face of outside aggression have all been local affairs involving small segments of the population operating in limited areas. When the conflict with outsider has involved the entire country and its aftermath], . . . the response has also been decidedly local, organized on tribal, clan, family, ethnic or sectarian lines and focused not on national but on local objectives."[McChesney 1999: 7]

Afghan nationalism, as it will be made clear, has drastic consequences for nation building and security both domestically and internationally. Domestically, it causes bloodshed and destruction and other miseries. Internationally, Afghan nationalism and divided loyalties allow neighboring countries and other foreigners to meddle in the internal affairs of the country as in the Russian (former Soviet Union) invasion and the subsequent civil war after the withdrawal of Russian forces, which allowed further bloodshed and destruction.

Afghan nationalism is a survival mechanism since the country is not and never has been a nation-state. In a nation-state, there is rule of law, equality, freedom of speech and assembly, checks and balances, protection of rights, and so on. Until Afghanistan becomes a nation-state, Afghan nationalism will remain a major obstacle to nation building and the creation of national unity. An understanding of Afghan nationalism is crucial to the reconstruction and building of democratic institutions in the country including building the Afghan National Army

(ANA) and the Afghan National Police (ANP) and Border Guards (BG).

Dimensions of Afghan Nationalism

What is the nature of Afghan nationalism? Prior to the invasion by the former Soviet Union in 1979, Afghans identified themselves with ethnicity or *qawm* (see Appendix), or sect and region. But the invasion and the subsequent civil war added another dimension: ideology. Thus Afghan nationalism now consists of ethnicity, sect, regionalism and ideology.

Ethnicity (*qawmparasti*)

The word *ethnicity* refers to language and race. "Ethnic group formation is based on a collective name, a common myth of descent, a shared history, a distinctive shared culture, association with a particular territory, and a sense of solidarity. It is on the basis of these features that one can distinguish ethnic groups from each other."[39] In Afghanistan, the word *qawm* is commonly used by all ethnic groups and implies more than ethnicity, tribe, and so on. Besides, since not all of Afghan society is tribal, the word *qawm* would be more accurate and comprehensive than *tribe* in the Afghan context. According to Olivier Roy, "A *qawm* is any segment of the society bound by close ties: it could be an extended family, a clan, an occupational group, or a village. A *qawm* is based on kinship and client-patron relations. Before being an ethnic group, it is a solidarity group, which protects its members from encroachments from the state and other *qawms* and includes the sense of lively competition between contenders for local supremacy."[40]

Afghans become aware of their ancestry at an early age. By the age of seven, a child knows whether he is Pashtun, Tajik, Hazara, or whatever. Ethnic groups differ in the way they speak, dress, eat, pray, and even where they bury their dead. Ethnic awareness early on is critical for survival in countries such as Afghanistan. One's ethnicity affects employment, education, marriage, social status, security, and other aspects of life in the country. In the West, on the other hand, ethnic identity is not so important. An American, for example, may not learn about his ancestry until college age. The reason is that he is American first and German, French, Swedish Italian, and so on as second. Ethnicity in the West has very little, if any, relevancy in employment, education, and other aspects of life because advancement and promotions are based on merits and qualifications. Neither does ethnicity have bearing when it comes to law reinforcement.

Ethnic loyalty (*qawmparasti*) and domination is an important aspect of Afghan nationalism. Of all the ethnic groups, the Pashtuns have been dominant since the inception of modern Afghanistan in 1747 when Ahmad Shah Durrani, a Pashtun, established the country. Ethnic conflicts also exist in individualistic societies such as the United States, but they do not result in the same level and devotion of violence as in the collectivistic countries such as Afghanistan. That is why to control the other ethnic groups, Pashtuns have used a variety of means including violence and direct attacks. Historically, the majority of ethnic conflicts have been between the Pashtuns and the minorities, especially the Hazaras and Tajiks.

In modern Afghanistan, there have been more conflicts between the Pashtuns and the Hazaras than between any two other ethnic groups in the country. King Abdul Rahman Khan (1880-1901) launched a major attack against the Hazaras in the 1880s killing hundreds, if not thousands, of them. "He gave much of their land to the Pashtun, made many of them slaves, and left them as the poorest of the four ethnic groups in Afghanistan."[41] In more recent times, Hafizullah Amin (September 14-December 27) sent thousands of Pashtuns to Bamiyan Province killing hundreds, including boys over the age of eight. The Pashtun Taliban (1992-2001), too, as part of their campaign of ethnic cleansing, killed hundreds of Hazaras in Bamiyan and Balkh provinces after the capture of Kabul in 1994. In Yakawlang and Bamiyan, for example, houses and shops were burned down and the areas were depopulated. An eyewitness, Sayed Abdul Hussain, a resident of Katakhana, Yakawlang, says during the Taliban attack:

> *When the Taliban came to Yakawlang, they took my young nephew out of his home. He was still wearing his white wedding clothes and his eyes still blackened with collyrium and his hands red with henna when he was gunned down. His mother and bride threw themselves on his bloodied body while the Taliban were whipping the women ... That scene is still fresh in my memory ... The Taliban came to our home and tied me up along with my three sons. Then they took us out of our home. Very soon, they moved us near a stream behind the Agsa Institute, where other innocent people were lined up. My sons told me to go and join the three elderly in the corner because they could not tolerate watching my execution, not knowing that I could not watch the execution of my eighteen-, twenty-, and twenty-five-year-old sons. All of a sudden, a Taliban came and moved me to the corner with the elderly. Then they began firing at my three sons and other twelve defenseless young boys. Within minutes, they all fell down on the ground like tree leaves. Then another Taliban came and shot at their heads.[42]*

This is only one example of what the Taliban did to the Hazaras in a small village. The same thing happened in other Hazara villages and towns in Hazarajat. In Mazr-e Sharif, too, the Taliban militia killed hundreds of Hazaras. It is worth noting that the Hazaras had also killed many Taliban previously when the latter attacked Mazar-e Sharif.

Prior to the Taliban when the Mujahideen came to power in 1992, bloody clashes took place between the Hazaras and other Shi'is and the Pashtuns of Abdurab Rasul Sayyaf's in Afshar, Kart-e Sakhi, and other districts west of Kabul. The clash in Afshar is said to have been very bloody and cruel resulting in many deaths that also included Shi'i women.

There have also been some clashes between Pashtuns and Tajiks, two of which are worth mentioning. One took place in 1929 when Mohammed Nadir Khan, a Pashtun, overthrew the Tajik government of Habibullah Kalakani (1929) with the support of thousands of Pashtun militias from the southeast. After capturing Kabul, he sent these militias to the Shumali Plain, north of Kabul and to the home of Habibullah Kalakani where hundreds of Tajik men were killed, their women taken as slaves, and their property in the form of cash, gold coins, and jewelry taken. The other major conflict between the Pashtun and the Tajik happened during the Taliban period. Like Mohammed Nadir Khan after the capture of Kabul, in 1994, the Taliban attacked the Shumali Plain killing hundreds, if not thousands, of Tajiks, burning their homes and destroying their orchards. Unlike Mohammed Nadir Khan though the primarily Pashtun Taliban practiced extreme ethnic cleansing in Shumali. It was during the Taliban rule that millions of Tajiks were displaced, forcing them to leave their homes and go to safer regions inside the country or outside to Iran and Pakistan.

In a conflict, members of one ethnicity tend to avoid fighting against members of their own group when an outsider is involved. For example, the Ghilzai and other Pashtun tribes did not confront the mostly Durrani Pashtun Taliban in the latter's attempts to bring the country under their control in early 1990s. There was little or no resistance in the south and east of the country where the Pashtuns are concentrated. Most of the fighting took place between the Taliban and Tajiks, Hazaras and other non-Pashtuns in Kabul and the northern and western provinces of Afghanistan where the non-Pashtuns reside. As another example, when the Mujahideen captured Bagram Air Base, north of Kabul, the Communist Tajiks and other non-Pashtuns officers did not fight the Mujahideen. Rather, they joined the the latter forces along ethnic lines. The Tajik and other non-Pashtun Communists joined forces with the late Ahmad Shah Massoud (a Tajik) and the Pashtun Communists with the Pashtun Gulbuddin Hekmatyar.

The Pashtun-dominated rulers of the country have depended on their fellow Pashtun groups and used one ethnic group against the other to stay in power. Until the Communist Coup of 1978, the majority of the officers and commanders in the military, police, intelligence, and other security forces were Pashtuns, but the majority of conscripts and rank and file were non-Pashtuns. There were two major reasons why the monarchies pursued this policy. One was to minimize the coming to power of the non-Pashtuns through military coups and other means. The other was to subjugate the population and prevent any uprisings and rebellions. To this end, the Pashtun-dominated governments would enroll more Pashtuns in the military high school and college and the police academy in Kabul so that upon graduation they would become officers. The Tajik enrollees in these institutions came second after the Pashtuns, followed by the other minority ethnic groups. The number of Hazara officers in the army and police was extremely small with none in the air force, where almost all the pilots were Pashtuns. And finally, the corps commanders were of a different ethnic background than the majority of the rank and file. For example, a Tajik would command mostly Pashtun troops or policemen, and a Pashtun would be made in charge of a corps dominated mostly by non-Pashtuns. In any uprisings in the Pashtun regions of the country, a non-Pashtun commander would be assigned to crush them, whereas Pashtun commanders would be sent to the non-Pashtun regions to deal with such problems.

The majority of the conscripts in the military and police, however, were non-Pashtuns. One reason is that some Pashtun ethnic tribes—those who had helped Mohammed Nadir Khan capture power from the Tajik ruler in 1929—did not have to serve the obligatory two-year military service. Another reason was that the Pashtuns make up about 40 percent of the population and the non-Pashtuns the other 60 percent. Because of divided loyalties, the non-Pashtun conscripts in both the police and armed forces would usually be assigned to the Pashto-speaking regions such as the south and the east while the Pashtun conscripts served their military duty in the non-Pashto-speaking provinces in the center, north, and west. Afghans tend not to fight their fellow ethnic groups due to their ethnic loyalties. It is important to note that the ethnic loyalties of the military and police have always been a serious problem for the central governments in Afghanistan, including the current government of Hamid Karzai.

After the Afghan Communist Coup of 1978 and the subsequent Soviet invasion in 1979, the makeup of the military and police force changed. More non-Pashtuns, especially the Hazara, found their way into the officer corps of the military and police for the first time in the history of modern Afghanistan.

Finally, the Pashtun monarchies employed fellow Pashtuns to guard the Royal Palace. However, these guards came from tribes other than their own—namely, the Ghilzai—because Pashtuns of their own tribe, Durrani, were not considered trustworthy. Historically, the Durranis have fought with each other for power. Therefore, the monarchies depended on tribes other than their own for protection. For example, the Yahya Dynasty employed the Ghilzai Pashtuns from Wardak, west of Kabul, as members of the Royal Guard—later renamed the Presidential Republican Guard. Aside from being tall and handsome, the Wardaks were very loyal to the royal family with no claims to the throne. They proved their loyalty to the monarchy during the Communist Coup of 1978. The Wardaks fought to the last man to defend the palace in Kabul where President Mohammad Daoud, his family, and other members of the royal family were residing.

It is not just the rulers who favor their ethnic fellows. Government officials, too, tend to be more favorable and sympathetic to their respective ethnic group at the expense of others. If the minister of education, for instance, is a Tajik, he tries to build more schools in his home province and employ more people from his own family and ethnic group with little or no attention to qualifications. The same is true with other ethnic groups. During the interim government of Hamid Karzai, I went to one of the ministries and noticed that most of the employees were from the minister's ethnic group, Hazaras. The same situation existed in the other ministries and institutions in the government. The Da Afghanistan Bank and the National Bank, as another example, were full of Pashtuns, mostly Ghilzais, because the general director was a Ghilzai Pashtun.

This is not, of course, anything new in the Afghan culture. The previous governments were a lot worse. When Mohammed Nadir, known as Nadir Khan, came to power on October 17, 1929, "the prime minister was the King's brother, Mohammad Hashim Khan; the Afghan minister of war, the King's other brother, Shah Mahmood Khan. Another brother, Shah Wali Khan, was *wakil-e slatanat* or crown prince; the minister of court was his cousin, Ahmad Shah Khan, . . . the king's another brother, Mohammad Aziz Khan, was ambassador to Moscow; his other cousins, Ahmad Ali Khan and Ali shah Khan, were respectively ambassador to Paris and London; and his sixteen-year old nephew, Assadullah Khan, was general of the Royal Guard."[43]

Ethnic favoritism also exists in some foreign firms and organizations in Afghanistan, perhaps without the explicit knowledge of their leaders. For example, in 2005 at the U.S. Embassy in Kabul, at least 80 percent of the Foreign Service Nationals (FSN) or locally hired employees, including those who taught Dari, were Pashtun. The reason is that the gentleman in charge of FSN personnel was a Pashtun. He must have helped his fellow Pashtuns get the jobs at the expense of Tajiks, Hazaras, and other ethnic groups. When an Afghan gets a job at a foreign firm, he or she tries to bring in as many of his or her relatives and fellow ethnic group as possible using a variety of means. One is to inform relatives or ethnic fellow about vacancies before anyone else finds out about them. Another is to coach his favorite person how to conduct himself in the interview and what kind of questions they might ask. And finally, the senior FSN usually recommends an ethnic fellow. I also noticed the same situation at some of the offices of the United Nations in Kabul. Given the group loyalties of Afghans, ethnic favoritism undoubtedly also existed in other embassies and foreign firms in Afghanistan.

Language is related to ethnicity and is a sensitive issue in Afghanistan. Unlike the West, where it is a means of communication and the key to learning, in Afghanistan people identify with language and use it as a tool for domination. Since Afghans identify with language, an attack on one's language is tantamount to an attack on the people who speak it.

Even though Dari is the interethnic language in the country, some Pashtun rulers have unsuccessfully tried to impose their language, Pashto, on the minority ethnic groups. To this end, a "Pashtunization" campaign was launched in the 1940s. One component of this campaign was to make Pashto the language of instruction in all the schools, including elementary schools, throughout the country. This was very harmful to the children of the minorities, especially to Uzbeks and Turkmens, as they were forced to study in a second language unrelated to theirs, instead of their mother language. However, after about ten years, the program ended because it had failed to achieve its purpose of making the minority children learn Pashto.

Still another aspect of this linguistic campaign was mandatory Pashto courses for non-Pashtun government employees. However, due to lack of motivation on the part of the learners, the absence of a pedagogically sound curriculum and textbooks, lack of qualified teachers, and valid and reliable tests, this program also failed. Not only were the students not learning much Pashto, their dislike of Pashto and the Pashtuns increased, damaging the national unity in the process. Nonetheless, Pashto courses were continued until the Communist Coup of 1978 because to the rulers the program was serving its purpose: punish and threaten the minorities.

Another objective of this language campaign was the purification of the Pashto language. To this end, the Pashto Society (Pashto Tolana) was established in 1940s. The primary target of this purification was to eliminate only Dari and Turkic loan words and give Pashto names to the existing Dari and Turkic ones. In Kabul, for instance, using names of Pashtun poets and rulers, certain Dari proper and common nouns were changed to Pashto: Khushal Maina, Wazir Akbarkhan Maina, Mirwais Maidan, and others. The existing Dari common nouns, such as *ketabkhana* (library) was changed to *ketabtoon*, even though native speakers of Pashto had been using such Dari words for centuries. Also, Turkic words such as *qaratapa* (black hill), on the border with Turkmenistan, was renamed *torghondi* (Black hill in Pashto), as well as others in northern and western provinces. Arabic, English, and Urdu loan words, however, were not touched. Replacing the existing Dari and Turkic words with Pashto, however, made the language difficult even for Pashtun children because most of them were coined by the Pashto society. The policy makers were oblivious to the fact that no language is pure, and attempts to purify language have failed all over the world. Once a word enters another language, either through borrowing or loan translation, it becomes part of that language.

It is important to note in this connection, however, that just as it is unnatural and unwise to purify Pashto of Dari words, it is also unnatural and unwise to purify Dari of Pashto loan words. Some Tajiks use Farsi (Iranian) words instead of the existing Pashto loan words in Dari. For example, using *danishga* instead of *pohantoon*, a Pashto loan word, for "university," or *danishkada* "college," instead of *pohanzai*, a Pashto word, is unnatural and unwise because these Pashto words have become part of the Dari language. This policy is also contrary to the principles of language change and language learning as it hinders communication and understanding.

In another measure to make Pashto superior and dominant, some previous Pashtun-dominated governments have tried to make the language the only official language of Afghanistan. The only other official language was Dari. All signs were supposed to be in Pashto. On the radio and television, too, Pashto news in prime time would be broadcast before the news in Dari. One newspaper, *Islah*, was entirely in Pashto and even Dari newspapers such as *Anis* were required to have some Pashto articles. The same was the case with magazines and other periodicals. The national identification booklet (*tazkera*) was and still is in Pashto as were all government official publications. At one time, there was talk of requiring all government communications to be in Pashto and making Pashto required of all new government employees.

When addressing the nation, government officials were supposed to deliver their speeches in Pashto. The only government "official" who always violated this rule, though, was none other than the late king, Mohammad Zahir Shah, himself. Even though a Pashtun, he could not give a formal speech in Pashto.

Still another measure to make Pashto the dominant language was the establishment of a new university in Jalalabad, Nangarhar Province. This served two purposes. One was to bar professors whose native language was not Pashto since the language of instruction was Pashto. Another was to enroll more Pashtun students.

With the Communist coup of 1978, however, the linguistic environment improved somewhat. Pashto courses for those government employees whose first language was not Pashto were abolished. Also, during the Russian occupation, minorities were allowed to have publications and radio programs in their native languages.

The linguistic environment improved further when Hamid Karzai came to power in 2001. The new constitution makes all languages of Afghanistan official. That means minority ethnic groups can have radio and television programs in their native languages. Additionally, for the first time in the history of modern Afghanistan, Uzbeks, Turkmens, Pashayees, and Baluchis can have their school textbooks in their native languages. Pedagogically, this is an excellent idea, but it is very costly and takes a while before such minorities can have educationally and linguistically sound textbooks and teachers' guides. Despite these linguistic improvements, language is and will be a sensitive issue in Afghanistan until the country moves in the direction of becoming a true nation-state.

Finally, aside from trying to make Pashto the lingua franca of the country, in the 1960s, the Pashtun-dominated government redrew the provincial borderlines in the country. The purpose of this strategy was twofold: to break up the Hazarajat and increase the number of Pashto-speaking provinces. As a result of this strategy, some Hazara regions were made part of a newly created province, Maidan-Wardak, a Pashto-speaking region west of Kabul. Other Hazara regions became part of Zabul, Helmand, Oruzgan, Baghlan, Parwan, and so on. Bamiyan was the only province with the Hazaras. Only later during the Karzai government was another Hazara-dominated region, Daikundi Province, created. This may not have happened if the second vice president was not a Hazara. Another non-Pashtun region that was made into a separate province during Karzai's reign is Panjshir, north of Parwan Province where Tajiks reside because the first vice president is a Tajik from Panjshir.

Aside from breaking up the Hazarajat, the redrawing of provincial borderlines also added to the number of Pashto-speaking provinces, thereby increasing Pashtun representation in the three branches of government, which meant more funds and public services for the Pashtuns. In the southeast, Paktia, a Pashto-speaking province, was made into three separate provinces of Paktia, Paktika, and

Khost. In the southwest, Kandahar, a Pashtun province, was made into three provinces: Kandahar, Helmand, and Oruzgan. Ghazni, mostly a Pashto-speaking region, was made into two provinces of Ghazni and Zabul. Logar, south of Kabul City and mostly a Pashto-speaking region, was made into a separate province, whereas the Dari-speaking region north of the capital city of Kabul (Saraykhaj, Estalif, Shakardara, Kalakan, and others) was kept as part of the Kabul province even though the latter is more populated than Logar.

Sectarianism (*mazhabgarayi*)

The second major aspect of Afghan nationalism is sectarianism, involving primarily Sunnism and Shi'ism. Most ethnic groups in Afghanistan are Sunni (80-85 percent), which include Pashtuns, Tajiks, Uzbeks, Turkmens, and others. The Shi'is (15-20 percent) include the Imamis or Twelvers and Ismailis or Seveners. The former believe in twelve Imams, an Arabic word meaning "leader," with Ali ibn Abutalib, cousin and son-in-law of the Prophet Mohammad, being the first, and Al-Montazer (Mehdi) the last. The Ismailis, on the other hand, believe in seven Imams with Ali being the first and Ismail the last. The Imamis mostly live in the Hazarajat (Bamiyan, Daikundi, Ghazni, Helmand, Ghorband, Parwan provinces) with some in Kabul and Herat. The Ismailis, on the other hand, reside mostly in Baghlan and Badakhshan provinces. The majority of the Hazara are Imami Shi'is with a small number of Sunnis living in Ghorband, Parwan Province.

Historically, as has been pointed out, the conflicts with Hazaras have been both ethnic and sectarian, mostly involving Pashtuns. The Pashtuns are the most orthodox among the Sunnis. This is why some, if not many, Pashtuns despise the Shi'is, especially the Hazaras. Some orthodox Pashtuns even consider them *kafir* or infidels.

There are several reasons why Pashtuns and Shi'is are sworn enemies. One is that most, if not all, Pashtuns despise Shi'i Iranians. Prior to the founding of modern Afghanistan in 1748, Mirwais Hotak, a Pashtun, had ruled part of Iran. Afterward, the Persian Nader Shah Afshar was in control of the western parts of Afghanistan, including Kandahar in the south in the 1740s. Another reason is that there are religious and cultural ties between Iranian and Afghan Shi'is. Most, if not all, Afghan Shi'i clerics have studied in Iran. During the Russian occupation, for example, Tehran provided military, political, and financial assistance to the Hazara and other Shi'i political parties in the country. In fact, most of the Shi'i parties had their headquarters in Iran during this period. During the civil war, too, the Shi'i parties received Iranian support against the Taliban and other Sunni parties in Afghanistan. Still another reason for the bad blood between the Shi'is and Pashtuns is that the former have suffered so many atrocities and injustices from some Pashtun-dominated regimes of Afghanistan. Finally, the Hazara have been victims of injustice and atrocities because the Pashtun rulers have accommodated the nomad Pashtuns in the Hazarajat region. Every spring the Pashtun nomads move westward to the Hazarajat for pastures to feed their sheep herds. This sometimes leads to conflicts between the local Hazaras and the traveling Pashtun nomads. In such conflicts, the Pashtun-dominated governments have supported the latter. Thus, nomadic pastures have also been a source of tension between the Pashtun and the Hazara.

Regionalism (*samtgarayi* or *watandari*)

The third dimension of Afghan nationalism is regionalism, which has existed in the culture for a long time. The Dari word *watandar* (compatriot), first and foremost, refers to one's place of birth and only after to the country as a whole. In fact, outside of the country, unless two individual Afghans are from the same region in Afghanistan, they tend not to refer to themselves as *watandar* (compatriots). Instead, they prefer saying, "We are from Afghanistan," rather than "We are compatriots."

Just as Afghans identify with ethnicity and sect, they also associate with their birthplace. Some choose their birthplace as their last name. Hence, Adul Ali Mazari (from Mazar-e Sahrif), Akhtar Mohammad Paktiawal (from Paktia), Mohammad Tahir Badakhshi (from Badakhshan), Mohammad Esmail Balkhi (from Balkh), Mohammad Omar Wardak (from Wardak), Dastagir Panjshiri (from Panjshir), and so on.

Afghans generally favor and trust people from their own region in employment, distribution of government funds, tests and exams, marriage, friendship or in minor and major conflicts. When the Taliban were in power, people from the Greater Kandahar region—currently Kandahar, Oruzgan, and Helmand provinces—held important senior posts in the regions under the Taliban control including the capital, Kabul. When in positions of power Afghans tend to provide more government assistance and even foreign aid to the region where they were born in providing scholarships, education, health and other benefits. For example, Panjshir, which was only a sub-governorship (*woluswali*), Parwan Province, prior to the overthrow of the Taliban, has been elevated to governorship (*welayat*). It now enjoys paved roads, clinics, a hospital, a university, secondary schools, and so on, enjoying the benefits and privileges of a full-fledged province. Now it has its own governor, annual budget, provincial council, departments of education, health, finance, and others. The primary reason is that the current vice president, Ahmad Zia

Massoud, and the speaker of parliament, Yunus Qanuni, and other officials in the Karzai government are from Panjshir. Without the influence of these figures, Panjshir would not have become a province.

Similarly, since important posts in the current government, including the presidency, are held by Pashtuns, more government and foreign funds are used in the reconstruction of the Pashto-speaking provinces, especially in the southwest and southeast of the country. The other provinces, in comparison, have received a lot less reconstruction funds and assistance.

In conflicts, too, Afghans take the side of the party from their respective region. In high school and university dorms where students from all ethnic groups and provinces of the country stay, if a fight breaks out between, say, a Kandahari and a Badakhshani, the students from these two provinces defend their respective compatriots. In political parties, the leadership is usually of the same region as that of the leader. For example, in Hizb-e Islami Gulbudin (HIG), the majority of the top positions were held by Pahtuns from Kunduz because Gulbuddin Hekmatyar, its leader, is from that province. Similarly, since Burhanuddin Rabbani was the leader of Jamiat-e Islami (JI), Badakhshis, or Badakhshanis held important positions in the party. In the Shura-ye Nizar, the Panjshiris held the majority of the senior positions because the late commander Ahmad Shah Massoud was a Panjshiri.

Ideology (*aqida*)

Ideology (*aqida*), the fourth dimension of Afghan nationalism, is a relatively recent phenomenon. The establishment of political parties in the nineteen sixties introduced foreign ideologies—Communism, Maoism, Islamism and nationalism—to the Afghan political discourse. Of all these ideologies, Marxism-Leninism and Islamism were intensified by the Communist Coup of 1978 and the subsequent Soviet invasion in 1979. Political parties were divided into those of the resistance and the promoters of Communism. In other words, it was Islam against atheism. The resistance Islamic parties (the Mujahideen, those who waged holy war or jihad) and the Communist parties were formed along ethnic, sectarian, and regional lines with the former opposing the Russians and the pro-Moscow installed government in Kabul and the latter defending it.

Almost all the Afghan political parties are formed on ethnic, sectarian, regional, and ideological lines. For example, during the Russian occupation the Sunni political parties had their bases of operations in Pakistan while the Shi'is were stationed in Iran. Of the seven Mujahideen parties in Pakistan, six of them were Pashtun and one Tajik. However, none of the political parties in Pakistan were entirely made up of one ethnic group. The Pashtun parties were about 80 percent Pashtun and the rest non-Pashtun. The same is true of the Tajik party in Pakistan with about 80 percent Tajik and the rest non-Tajiks. Almost all the Shi'i political parties consisting of Hazara, Qizilbash and others were stationed in Iran whose official religion is Shi'i Islam.

The Communist parties in the government, too, were also formed along ethnic lines. The Khalq (people's) party was mostly Pashtun whereas the Parcham (banner) party was mostly Tajik. It is also important to note that these Sunni and Shi'i Mujahideen groups fought the Russian and Afghan troops separately with each party waging its own battles. Sometimes they even fought against each other rather than with the Soviets and local Communists. The clashes between Ahmad Shah Massoud and Gulbuddin Hekmatyar forces during this period are well-known.

It is due to Afghan nationalism that there are ethnic, sectarian, regional and ideological cliques in all the branches of the government at all levels. Aside from the Mujahideen Islamists and fundamentalists, some former Communists and nationalists are also in the executive, judiciary, and legislative branches of the current government, forming their own ideological, ethnic, sectarian, and regional cliques which are constantly engaged in jockeying for power. For example, on one level, in the current government, especially in the executive branch where most of the power lies, the Pashtuns are trying to marginalize the non-Pashtuns, especially the Tajiks, and vice versa. On another level, among the Pashtuns, the Durranis are trying to undermine their rival Ghilzais and vice versa. The non-Pashtuns, too, are trying to weaken the Pashtuns. Among the non-Pashtuns, the Tajiks are trying to undermine the Hazara, Uzbeks, and other minorities and vice versa.

Regionally, too, there is rivalry between the Pashtun Durrani in the southwest and the Pashtun Ghilzai in the southeast and the east. Among the non-Pashtuns, the non-Panjshiris try to weaken the Panjshiris.

Ideologically, too, the secularists—Western-educated and former Communist Afghans—are trying to weaken the Islamists and other Mujahideen. The Mujahideen, who dominate all the branches of the Karzai government, are hard at work to discredit and marginalize Western educated and other secularists, especially those holding key positions in the government. A case in point is Dr. Rangin Dadfar Spanta, minister of foreign affairs and a secularist. In the summer of 2007, the Afghan Wolusi Jirgah, dominated by the Mujahideen, voted to suspend him as minister of foreign affairs of the Karzai government; but Karazi opposed his ouster. As of this writing, the issue has not been resolved yet.

The same group loyalties also exist in the media, in both print and electronic. Some television and radio stations as well as newspapers and magazines support their affiliated groups and discredit their rivals.

This makes it critical to identify the ethnic, sectarian, regional, and ideological affiliations of Afghans in the government and in the media. It is important to keep in mind that Afghan culture is based on relationships. One cannot fully understand Afghans without knowledge of such relationships and ties. That is why when a government official is appointed to a position of power, the employees would like to learn his family, ethnicity, region, sect, and ideological ties so they can deal with him accordingly. An understanding of the group affiliation of Afghan officials is also crucial for foreigners dealing with Afghans.

Historically, of all the dimensions of Afghan nationalism, ethnicity has been most dangerous as it has led to many conflicts, some very bloody and destructive. When one of these dimensions becomes a hot issue, it supersedes the others. For example, during the Soviet occupation, ideology (Islamism versus Communism) became a hot issue. Consequently, ethnicity, sect, and other dimensions of Afghan nationalism were left aside. Thus, Afghans were divided into two major camps: the Islamic Mujahideen and pro-Moscow Communists. The former fought against the Soviet occupation and the latter tried to defend it. However, after the withdrawal of Soviet forces, ethnicity, sect, and region became dominant, and Afghans fought among themselves along these lines. Most of the Pashtuns united with the Taliban against the non-Pashtuns, although the Taliban conflict with the Hazaras also involved sectarianism.

Aside from foreign invasion, inter-Afghan nationalism can intensify and lead to bloodshed when the central government is weak and foreign or neighboring powers are involved. There are cases in Afghan history to support this claim. For instance, during the strong central government of Abdul Rahaman Khan at the end of the eighteenth century and also during the Musahibeen rule (1929-1967), interethnic tension did not get out of control to cause a civil war. In both cases, the central governments were strong. However, as has been pointed out earlier, during the reign of Habibullah Kalakani (January-October 1929, when Mohammed Nadir came to power, and later on when the Mujahideen came to power (1992-2001) the ethnic conflict led to civil wars because in both cases the central governments were weak and foreigners were involved. The involvement of the British in Mohammed Nadir Khan's case, and the regional and neighboring countries, especially Pakistan, al-Qaeda, and Iran, in the Mujahideen's case, indicate that foreigners engage in meddling in the internal affairs of the country when there is a weak central government.

Nation-State (*Dawlat-e Milli*)

The previous discussion on Afghan nationalism gives rise to an important question: why are Afghans first loyal to their family, ethnicity, sect, region, or ideology and only secondly to the country as a whole? The answer quite simply is that Afghanistan is not, and has never been, a nation-state (*dawlat-e milli*). A political boundary, a constitution, a national anthem, a government, diplomatic missions, and elections do not necessarily make a country a nation-state: they are only symbols.

The phenomenon of nation-states has its roots in the West. It took the West centuries to establish their nation-states. Even the United States was originally not a nation-state until after the Civil War of 1861-1865. The Reformation, the Enlightenment, and the Industrial

Revolution were crucial to the establishment of nation-states in the West. In the Reformation, which took place in Europe in the sixteenth century, people protested against the domination of the Catholic Church and its doctrine. The motivation for this movement was an emphasis on spiritual and individual freedoms and separation of church and state, leading eventually to secularism. Later, during the Enlightenment of the eighteenth century, philosophers such as John Locke, Francis Bacon, Benjamin Franklin, Thomas Jefferson, and others played a significant role in creating the conditions for the development of nation-states. As a result of this movement, secularism was further strengthened, and people began critical analysis of social, religious, economic, and political issues. This too, further increased individual rights and human dignity and respect. Finally, in the industrial revolution of the nineteenth century, the invention of the steam engine and the improvement of the various types of machinery and their methods of use allowed for the development of individual freedoms.

These movements in Eastern Europe and North America put an end to most totalitarianism and dictatorships and replaced them with democracies. This is why people in those regions have a government of the people, by the people, and for the people. In such countries, people have rights; there is freedom of speech, assembly, and religion; there is a free press; there are political parties and fair and free elections; there is a separation of church and state; the powers of the three branches of government are controlled through checks and balances; pluralism, tolerance, and transparency are practiced. In short, there is democracy, freedom, and the rule of law. It is under these circumstances that people rally around the constitution, the flag, and the national anthem instead of family, ethnicity, sect, region, or ideology.

The concept of "nation-state" has been tried in several Islamic countries in the Middle East and other parts of the world. The first Islamic country to adopt this concept was Turkey. In 1923, Mustafa Kemal Ataturk ("ataturk" means "Father of Turkey" in Turkish), known as Ataturk in Afghanistan and some other countries, abolished the Islamic caliphate, separated the church from the state, established political parties, wrote a constitution, and formed a parliament. The Turks rallied behind their language, constitution, flag, and national anthem. Thus, Mustafa Kemal laid the foundation of a modern nation-state for the first time in the Islamic world. This is why Turkey is the most democratic Islamic country in the Middle East. Some other Islamic leaders tried to follow suit, namely, Reza Shah of Iran and Shah Amanullah (1919-1929) of Afghanistan but with less success.

It is important to note that *nation-state* or *nationhood* are relative terms. There are degrees of nationhood. Even in America, the cradle of democracy, women could not vote until the constitution was amended in 1920; and as yet, no woman or minority has been elected president. Women, on the average, still make less money than men. In short, some countries are more democratic than others, and some are not democratic at all. That is why in some countries, nationhood has deep roots while in others, it has shallow or no roots at all. After Turkey, in the Middle East and Southwest Asia, the nation-state which has the deepest roots is Iran. Iran fought an eight-year war with Iraq, but it did not fall apart even though the latter had the backing of the Arab countries and a superpower, the United States. Afghanistan, however, fell apart after the withdrawal of Soviet forces in 1988 partly because nationhood has no roots there. In the 1920s, Shah Amanullah, imitating Mustafa Kemal, tried to lay the foundations of a nation-state in Afghanistan, but his democratic reforms failed and he lost his throne in the process. The nation-state has no roots in the Arab world with the exception of Egypt where its roots are very shallow. In Pakistan, too, nationhood has shallow roots; if the Kashmir issue is resolved, it will easily disintegrate. The civil war in Iraq is another good example of what happens to a non-nation-state in a crisis.

Collectivism in the Workplace

It is essential for the Westerner to identify ties of Afghan supervisors, coworkers, and subordinates: family, ethnicity, sect, region, and ideology (Islamists, secularists, nationalists). Such understanding is crucial in understanding their behavior, tendencies, and attitudes. As a supervisor, it is also important to maintain ethnic balance by hiring qualified people from all ethnic groups, not just one or two. It is not hard to find qualified individuals in almost all the Afghan ethnic groups. Additionally, favoritism should be avoided in the workplace: all subordinates need to be treated equally. Promotions and salary raises should be based on performance and other objective criteria. Teamwork and competition need to be emphasized to the subordinates from the very beginning as these qualities are almost nonexistent in the culture due to Afghan nationalism, uncertainty avoidance, and other cultural traits. In short, being fair and firm is a good rule of thumb for the creation of a productive work environment.

The Westerner also needs to keep in mind that befriending an Afghan is like becoming a member of his or her family. As such, the Westerner is expected to behave like a family member. As has been pointed out in this chapter, Afghans expect loyalty, support and favoritism, and others from a friend. Afghans usually do not keep personal and business matters separate. Not only does the Westerner need to prevent such favoritism in the workplace, but he must also avoid falling into this loyalty trap himself. It is a good idea to make it clear to all the Afghan subordinates from the beginning that there is zero tolerance for favoritism of any kind in the workplace. Finally, the Westerner should never lend money to coworkers and subordinates. Providing cash to a poor Afghan in an emergency is fine as long as it is not a loan. Afghans never forget favors in times of need. The bottom line is that, as a rule of thumb, it is not a good idea to do business with a coworker, a subordinate or a supervisor as it is to stay away from politics and religion in the workplace.

Conclusions

The fact that nation-building took so long to develop in the West does not, however, mean it should necessarily take developing countries that long to become nation-states. India is a case in point. That country is now a giant democracy, even though it became independent only in 1947. For the establishment of a nation-state, certain conditions are necessary. One is that democracy should come from the bottom up rather than from the top down.

Elections—presidential, parliamentary, mayoral, and others—do not necessarily mean there is democracy in a country if they are not truly free and fair. Hosni Mubarak of Egypt, for example, always wins the presidential elections, and his party is victorious in parliamentary and local elections as does Bashar al-Alasad of Syria. The same is true with the newly created states in Central Asia. The July parliamentary elections in Turkey, on the other hand, were free and fair. The point being made is that only in countries with deep roots of nationhood are elections relatively free and fair.

Toward a Nation-State

Prior to the establishment of the interim government in Afghanistan in 2001, there was a lot of talk about the future form of government. These discussions revolved around two forms of government to ensure stability and bring about democracy in Afghanistan: a strong central government and some type of Federalism.

Establishing a central government is no longer viable in Afghanistan. In the past, whenever there was a strong central government, it was due to the existence of the following prerequisites: there was autocratic rule; the national army was strong; most of the Pashtuns and all the non-Pashtuns were disarmed; the majority of the people were unaware of their rights, and their political consciousness was low; and, most importantly, there was very little, if any, foreign meddling in the internal affairs of the country. The Soviet invasion and the subsequent civil war have changed Afghan society and the geopolitical situation of Afghanistan, making the establishment of a strong government extremely difficult, if not impossible. Additionally, as Nazif Shahrani correctly states, "The painful lesson of Afghanistan's history has been that strong centralized government in any form will only lead to hegemony by one group, whether ethnic, linguistic, or religious, and abuse by ruling group at the expense of justice for all citizens of Afghanistan."[44] That is why, unlike the past, ethnic tensions are so deep now that the Pashtuns or any other ethnic group for that matter can no longer dominate the political scene. Those who support a strong central government, Afghan and foreigners, for Afghanistan believe that since the Pashtuns have dominated the political scene in the past, they should also dominate in the future. Similarly, the Sunni Arabs, who—until 2003—had dominated the political scene in Iraq, are for a strong central government, whereas the Arab Shi'is and Sunni Kurds favor Federalism and a weak central government.

The fact is that, those days when one ethnic group was more equal than others are gone. The genie is out of the bottle and the establishment of a strong central government is no longer viable in Afghanistan. If it were, Hamid Karzai, backed by tens of thousands of the coalition and ISAF forces, would have been able to establish one by now.

Therefore, some form of Federalism is necessary to reduce ethnic tensions, prevent another civil war and keep Afghans united. If the people of each province chose their governors—provincial and district—judges and chiefs of police and other public officials, the security situation would improve and reconstruction efforts would have positive results. This in turn would also be a major step in the direction of making Afghanistan a nation-state. To do so, however, would require that the constitution be amended and the provincial boundaries redrawn, among others. The best time to make the change is now when the coalition forces led by the United States and ISAF troops are still in Afghanistan. This is because Afghans, especially many if not all, of the Pashtuns, are not willing to share power. They tend to fight it out until one ethnic subjugates the opposing ones. This is exactly what was happening during the Taliban. Never mind if it was with the backing of al-Qaeda, Pakistan, and some Arab countries. If it had not been for 9/11, the Taliban movement would have conquered the entire country; Ahmad Shah Massoud, the only opposition commander, had been just assassinated. Hence, establishing some type of Federalism requires the involvement of the United Nations and the rest of the international community.

In the meantime, however, some measures could be taken to reduce ethnic tensions and make Afghanistan more democratic. One is to develop the existing system of electing *maleks* and *wakils* and to hold mayoral and gubernatorial elections. There is also the democratic practice of *jirgahs* (assembly), which could be made more systematic and efficient. The tradition of calling a *jirga* is a long tradition in Afghanistan. It is more common among the Pashtuns but is also practiced by other ethnic groups (*qawms*). The primary purpose of calling a *jirgah* is to resolve disputes or deal with pressing issues. It is used at all levels from intra- and inter-family to intra- and inter-*qawm* to national levels. *Jirgahs* at the national level are called *loya jirgah*s or "grand assemblies." Prior to the adaptation of "parliament" from the West, Afghan rulers would call such grand jirgahs to deal with national issues. Democratically elected, members of *jirgahs* are the elders and other trusted individuals in the community. Decisions made at a *jirgah* are fair and binding. That is why the Pashtuns prefer *jirgah*s to government courts, which are usually corrupt, unfair, cumbersome, time-consuming, and costly.

Another measure is to maintain ethnic balance in the government, especially the executive and judiciary branches where most of the positions are filled by appointments. For example, the cabinet should be 40 percent Pashtun, 27 percent Tajik, 17 percent Hazara, 9 percent Uzbek, and so on. Other government positions, too, should also reflect this ethnic composition. The selection from each ethnic group should be based on qualifications. In other words, the best of each ethnic group should be chosen to represent their ethnic group in the government. Doing so would not only promote national unity in the government but would also result in more competent officials who could serve the people better. However, to implement this plan, an overall agreement on the percentage of each ethnic group would be necessary. This quota system is doable just as decreeing 25 percent females in the present parliament is. Ethnic tension is a reality that must be dealt with. By making and talking about it as a taboo will not make it go away. In fact, not talking about it is more damaging to national unity.

Finally, there is a need for balancing how the government and foreign funds are allocated in the country. At the moment, there is a lot of resentment on how the reconstruction funds are distributed. To the non-Pashtun, most of the government and foreign funds are allocated in the south and east of Afghanistan, where the Pashtun reside. Controlling this practice and promoting ethnic balance in institutions strengthens national unity and moves the country in the direction of becoming a nation-state.

Food for Thought

(1) Are ANA and ANP loyal to President Karzai and the central government? Why, or why not?

(2) Can loyalty to the state be instilled in the army and the police during and after training? How?

(3) Are the border guards stationed on the eastern borders of Afghanistan capable of preventing the Taliban and al-Qaeda from entering the country, knowing that they are mostly from that area? Why, or why not?

(4) Would it be a good idea to send non-Pashtun ANA and ANP to the south and east to fight the insurgency? Explain your answer. Why, or why not?

(5) What do you think will happen once the coalition and NATO forces leave Afghanistan? Explain.

(6) What is the ethnic, regional, sectarian and ideological makeup of the ANA and ANP?

(7) What is the ethnic and ideological makeup of the executive, legislature, and judiciary branches in the Karzai government?

(8) Why is it that the same personalities who came to power in the interim government of Hamid Karzai are still in power?

(9) Why has President Karzai been unable to establish a strong central government?

(10) Has the allocation of funds for reconstruction from foreign donations to Afghanistan been balanced?

(11) It has been reported that almost 40 percent of foreign donations has been misdirected or embezzled. What can the international community do to prevent this from happening?

(12) What criteria are used to subcontract the various parts of the reconstruction projects to NGOs and others?

(13) What are the pros and cons of Federalism for Afghanistan?

(14) The majority of Pashtuns seem to be against Federalism for Afghanistan while the minorities are for it. Why?

(15) Aside from distance, what are the other reasons why the Taliban are mostly active in the south and the east of the country?

(16) Why are hospitality and revenge important traits of Afghan culture?

(17) The number of civilian casualties due to U.S.-led coalition and NATO attacks on terrorist targets is on the rise. According to United Nations sources, during the first six months of 2007, 600 civilians have been killed in Afghanistan as a result of

clashes between the Taliban and foreign troops Since revenge is a significant part of Afghan society, what are the likely consequences for the coalition and NATO forces?

(18) Why is it that Osama bin-Ladin has not been captured even though the bounty on his head amounts to millions of dollars?

CHAPTER 4

Masculinity or the Gender Gap

The two pleasures of life are women and teeth.
—Afghan proverb

Introduction

In late May or early June of 2007, Malalai Joya, a female representative from Farah province was suspended from the Wolusi Jirgah (House of Representatives). The reason was that she had referred to the Wolusi Jirgah as a "stable" implying that its members were like animals. She had also used harsh words against the Mujahideen leaders. For example, in the Loya Jirgah (grand assembly in Pashto) two years ago she had said that some jihad leaders were "war criminals" who must be put on trial. On 9 June of 2007, she repeated the same words in an interview with Tolo Television. While to some Afghan intellectuals and her followers her action was courageous, Malalai Joya violated an important Afghan cultural rule: only men can be assertive in Afghan society. This issue relates to the fourth dimension of culture—Masculinity or the Gender gap.

Masculinity (MAS)[45] or the gender gap involves the equality, or lack of it, between women and men in societies. Just as there are degrees of power distance, uncertainty avoidance and individualism, masculinity, too, has degrees; it can be high or low in different cultures. Afghanistan is a high MAS culture, whereas the United States is low. MAS correlates positively with power distance and uncertainty avoidance but negatively with individualism. Thus as a high MAS society, Afghanistan is also on the high side of power distance and uncertainty avoidance but on the low side of individualism.

While democratic societies in the West have made a great deal of progress in power distance, uncertainty avoidance and individualism, the gender gap is still problematic in these societies. In the United States, for example, women could not vote until 1920, and no woman has yet become vice president or president.

MAS involves the duality of male and female. If the duality of life and death is nature's number one law, the duality of male and female is its number two. Human societies, regardless of their complexity and age, must deal with this issue, resulting in sex-role systems that are formed by cultural norms. The reason for the existence of sex duality is that in procreation, women bear children and men beget them. It is here, though, that almost all differences due to the laws of nature end and differences of cultural norms in the form of sex roles begin. It is said that men are taller and stronger than women. This, however, is not an absolute fact since there are many women who are as tall and strong as many men. What is true, then, is that statistically men are stronger than women. Sex roles in society are due more to social rather than natural or biological factors. [Hoffstede 1980: 177-8]

MAS refers to the dominant sex role patterns played by men and women in most traditional and modern societies. Men usually engage in behavior associated in their society with masculinity, while women behave in ways associated with femininity. Masculinity usually involves assertiveness, whereas femininity is associated with nurturance. However, men do not always behave on the masculine side or women on the feminine. Statistically, men tend to be more assertive and women more nurturing. However, the behavior of men is not always assertive nor that of women always nurturing.

It is important to note, though, that assertiveness and nurturance are not fundamental aspects of personality. Both are learned interpersonal interactions appropriate in the society. Assertiveness and nurturance have their own attributes in the home and the workplace.

While assertiveness and nurturance have some common characteristics in the national culture, they differ somewhat in the home and the workplace. Based on my observations and knowledge of Afghan culture, male assertiveness generally involves aggressiveness, bravery, endurance, leadership, power, dominance, and independence. Female nurturance, on the other hand, is characterized by submissiveness, patience, tenderness, and affection.

Assertiveness in the workplace is associated with management, leadership, advancement, power, earnings, recognition, independence, endurance, and loyalty (ethnic, regional, sectarian, and ideological). Nurturance, on the other hand, refers to patience, obedience, emotion, yielding, submissiveness, and tenderness.[46]

How Afghans Cope with Masculinity

Sex roles are learned early in life in the family and are reinforced in schools and other social institutions. Language, literature, education, religion, the family, employment, and other social organizations reflect sex role patterns in Afghan society.

Language and Literature

Language is a reflection of a people's experiences and culture. Dari, for example, makes a distinction between man (*mard*) and woman (*zan*) as well as between feminine (*mada / muanus*)[47] and masculine (*nar / muzakar*). Unlike Pashto and English, Dari has no personal pronouns distinguishing sex. However, the third person singular pronoun /uw/ (he/she) refers to a male unless it is specified.

Both the vocabulary of a language and the grammar reflect the culture. In grammar, one can observe cultural attitudes and beliefs with regard to gender. In the Dari language, actions related to women are in the passive voice. In passive voice, the subject is the receiver of the action. For example, "*Zan neka mesha*" "Girls get married," or "*Dokhtar toy / arusi mesha.*" (Girls get wedded). The word '*mesha*' (become) expresses the passive voice in Dari. For men and boys, however, the active voice using the verb *mekona* (he/she **does**) is employed. Thus, "*Mard toy / arusi mekona*" (Men do wedding/marriage), or "*bacha toy / arusi mekona*" (Boys wed). In sexual relationships, men are always the "doers" and women the "receivers," or "givers." For example, "Men kiss" (*Mard mach / bowsa mekona*) but "Women give kisses" (*Zan mach / bowsa meta*).

There are no words for "rape" either in Dari or in Pashto. The phrase "sexual attack" (*tajawuz-e jensi*) is used but not in the context of marital rape. To an Afghan raping one's wife is nonsense. Men do "it" whenever they feel like. It does not matter whether she likes it or not. If a wife went to court and complained, the judge would laugh and tell her not to make a fool of herself. For the same reason, Pashto and Dari have no word for "foreplay." This is because females are perceived as property and sex objects for the pleasure of men. There is no word for "dating" either. Nor is there any word for "boyfriend" or "girlfriend" because of the absence of the dating custom in the Afghan culture. Males can have only male friends or *rafiq* and females have female friends or *khwarkhanda*. In other words, *rafiq* is understood to mean only a male friend of a man and *khwarkhanda* means a female friend of a woman.

When I went to the United States for the first time in 1962, another Afghan and I had to fill out various forms at Columbia University in New York City. One of the forms had three boxes under the "marital status": married, separated, and divorced. My friend marked the "separated" box. When I told him to mark the "married" box, he said, "No, I'm separated; I'm here in America and my wife is in Afghanistan." In Afghanistan, one is either single, married, or divorced from; there is no such thing as "separated," even though Islam recognizes a separation period for the purpose of reconciliation. The national identity booklet (*tazkera-ye nefoos*), too, has only the categories of "single" (*mujarad*) and "married" (*mutahil*), omitting the third, "divorced" (*talaq*) because as it will be made clear, Afghan society looks down upon divorce.

Still another linguistic phenomenon is that women are defined only in relation to men. The English word *queen* is defined in relation to the king as *shah-khanum*, a compound noun meaning "the king wife". It is the same with the word *princess* whose equivalent in Dari is *shah-dukht* (the king daughter). However, the words for *king* and *prince* are single words rather than phrases, namely, *shah* and *shahzada* respectively.

Dictionaries, too, reflect bias against women. For example, according to Farayba Rafugaran,[48] the *Dehkhuda Dictionary* devotes ten and a half lines to the definition and description of *man* but only six and a half to that of *woman*. Additionally, the definitions and descriptions provided for men are generally positive and those for women negative. Thus, *man* is defined as "a male, a human, a single individual, a person, and a human being." A *woman*, on the other hand, is defined as "the opposite of man, a married, or single individual." On the social role of men, the dictionary says, "men rule, fight; they are understanding, get bloody, take blame, die and revitalize; they are in charge, struggle with death, keep their words; want their names to be immortal; have good judgment; speak well; want to be self sufficient; want friendship and love; want to be in control ; help the needy; are artists and writers; seek knowledge; suffer, work and get suspicious. Women are married, single, pregnant, impure, not virgin; they are beauticians, prostitutes, widows, adulterers, wizards, witches."[49]

Dari literature, too, is mostly negative about women. Both verse and prose, especially the classics, portray women as cunning, satanic, unfaithful, evil, emotional, and dishonest among others and advise men how to control them.[50]

Imam Mohammad Ghazali, for instance, on the characteristics of women writes, "God punished women because of Eve's disobeying God and eating from the wheat tree . . . [Thus] Women have . . . bad habits similar to pigs, monkeys, dogs, snakes, mice, scorpions, pigeons, fox and sheep."[51] Mawlana Nizami, in a poem, says, "There are thousands of women; a woman does not keep her promise; a woman is with you when she cannot find another lover; as soon as she finds another she no longer stays with you; this is what women do and their story of charm and deceit is long."[52] Another poet, Nasir Khusraw, in one of his poems, warns men about women and says, "Don't you ever listen to women; try to always keep them silent; they defy logic and religion; why should I go on their path? Don't shoulder the burden of woman and wealth;

abandon both."[53] Sheikh Sa'adi (Muslih-ud-Din Mushrif-ibn-Abdullah), in his *Gulistan,* says, "A bad woman is like Hell [in this world] in the company of a good man."

However, some limited verse and prose in classical literature have positive themes for women. Some poets advise men to be nice to women. For example, Mawlana Jalal-ad-Din Muhammad Rumi says, "The Prophet said women would overcome men; then the ignorant overcome women because the former have the nature of an animal"[54] "A man who has a good and pious woman in his house is in Paradise [in this world] because good women protect religion from what is religiously prohibited"; "Two kinds of people will go to Paradise: a man who loves his wife and she loves him; they both go to heaven" ; "You should know that women are good but their number is small. And the world exists because of women"; "And there are some women who are a hundred times wiser than men."

A few women, too, engage in counterattacks to improve their image. For example, Rabi'a, an Arab woman, is quoted as saying, "Women have three virtues that men do not. Firstly, there are no effeminates among women as this is a characteristic of men. Secondly, all the prophets, martyrs, and the pious were nourished in women's bellies and nurtured beside them. Thirdly, no woman has claimed to be god as this impoliteness is man's habit."[55]

The fact that this Arab woman defends women raises the question why the classical literature—verse and prose—quoted above paint a negative image of women. There are at least two reasons. One is that almost all of these writers were men, which signifies male domination in society. The other reason is that classical literature was produced almost entirely under the royal patronage of kings and emperors, most of whom had concubines and female slaves in addition to wives. And finally, women were kept illiterate.

Folk literature too, is mostly against woman, including proverbs and folk songs. According to Jalal Satari, "Of the 31 Farsi proverbs gathered on women the majority were mostly slanderous."[56] In the negative proverbs and sayings common in Afghanistan, women are sex objects, property, or evil as the following proverbs exemplify, "The pleasures of life are women and teeth." (sex object); "Women, land and jewelry are one's chattel (property); "Being away from women is being away from the devil on earth and the sky[above]"; "Women have [even] fooled the Satan"; "Women are disloyal"; and "Women are mentally deranged." A few proverbs are positive: "A woman is one's partner for life" and "Life without women is impossible."

In folkloric songs and legends, too, women are described as cunning and sex objects with the emphasis more on wedding and conjugal union than on love and affection. Faiz Karizi, a popular Afghan folk singer, in one of his songs, says "You are like a rose for me to smell; when would I marry you?" Some of the legends and stories talk about how cunning and deceitful women are as in *Shahnama, Warq-wu Gulshah, Yousuf Zolaikha,* and so on. It is not just language and literature that show the superiority of man to woman. Religion, too, plays its role in establishing sex roles and gender perception in Afghan society.

Religion

While mainstream Islam limits women's rights somewhat, it is mostly religious extremism and cultural traditions that damage the status of women in Afghanistan. In other words, the real problem is Islamic fundamentalism with its strict and narrow interpretation of Islam and the patriarchic view of society and the high level of MAS. Studies show, according to Hofstede, that there is a correlation between religiosity and MAS. Catholics are masculine, whereas Protestants are more feminine.[57] In other words, the more fundamentalist sects tend to be more MAS, to the detriment of women's rights, than are moderates. Whether Christian, Jewish, or Muslim, the more religious individuals are on the masculine side and less religious ones on the feminine side. Although studies on how fundamentalist Muslims and moderate Muslims view women have not been done in Afghanistan, it is more likely for the former to be masculine and the latter to be feminine. Put differently, Islamists are more opposed to women's rights than non-Islamists. As will be made clear, the situation of women has deteriorated since the Mujahideen and the Taliban came to power in Afghanistan.

Sex role issues in Islam revolve around marriage, divorce, inheritance, court witnessing, education, and employment.

Issues related to marriage include polygamy, arranged marriage, emergency marriage, and marriage age. Most Afghans are monogamous, but some are also polygamous (perhaps 1 percent). Islam allows a man to have up to four wives at one time provided they are all treated justly and he can afford it. The Qur'an says, "If you are afraid of being just, then one is sufficient."[58] Additionally, polygamy is not obligatory in Islam. "Only when it is necessary, in emergency and for the sake of God (orphans and war prisoners) men can have more than one wife."[59] In Shi'i jurisprudence, polygamy is discouraged because it is almost impossible to meet the criterion of being just. But Sunni jurisprudence does not seem to oppose it publicly. One reason may be that, unlike the Shi'is, *sighah* or temporary marriage is not practiced among the Sunnis. In sighah, a man can marry a woman for as short period as one hour. In Arabic this type of marriage is called "nikah mut'ah" which literally means "marriage for pleasure".

In Afghanistan, polygamy usually occurs when a man is rich and influential, the wife cannot bear sons, there is an emergency, or a combination of these. It is usually the rich and powerful who have more than one wife because getting married costs a great deal in Afghanistan where most people live in poverty. In addition to the expenses of engagement, one expenditure item is the *mahr* (dowry), which is required in Islam. Mahr is usually in the form of cash (*mu'ajal*) and real estate (*muajal*) to be collected only after the separation of the couple. This is required in Islam to provide security for the woman in the future. The other, and a more immediate problem, however, is the bride-price (*towyana*); although there are other expenses in the form of jewelry, clothing, live music, food, and so on that can amount to hundreds of thousands of afghanis (fifty afghanis is about one U.S. dollar and the average monthly salary of a government employee is fifty U.S dollars). Thus for most Afghan men, it is the cost of marriage that prevents them from having a second wife; only those who can afford it take a second or third wife.

Aside from wealth and power, sometimes, Afghan men also take a second wife when the first wife cannot bear a son. To the parents, especially the father, it is a son who is more dear and valuable than a daughter. Lack of sons is a loss of status for a woman. It is shameful for the wife first to fail in her duty to produce a son and then to have her husband bring another wife into her household.

Aside from the lack of having a son, Afghans also remarry when a male member in the family passes away at a relatively young age. Older widows usually do not remarry; but it is customary in Afghan culture, especially in the countryside and among the uneducated, for a male family member—married or single—to marry his brother's wife upon the latter's death. This kind of emergency marriage is more common among the Pashtuns in Afghanistan than other ethnic groups.

There are several reasons for this cultural tradition. Although in Islam, under certain conditions, a widow can have custody of her young children; they usually stay with the father's family unless the deceased is very poor or has no siblings to take care of the orphans. One reason orphans stay in the father's family involves the well-being of the children. Another is the belief that the children are best taken care of if they stay with their father's relatives. Still, it is considered shameful for the family if the widow remarries into another family, thus damaging the family honor. Finally, and perhaps most importantly, by keeping the orphans in the family, no wealth leaves the household and the line (ancestry) is kept "pure." The dowry and inheritance the widow and her children are entitled to can amount to a lot of money if the deceased was rich.

In such marriages, the age of the deceased's brother is not an issue. Sometimes the age difference can be huge, which is usually disadvantageous to the woman. The ultimate goal is to keep the widow in the family regardless of how she feels about the arrangement.

Another Afghan cultural tradition that violates the rights of women is *badal* (lit. exchange) or blood price. According to this tradition, more common among the Pashtun tribes, women are married off to settle feuds. If, for example, someone from another family commits murder, the family of the culprit must give a girl in marriage to the family member of the victim's in compensation for the shed blood. On occasions, this compensation may also take the form of cash. The goal in either case is to prevent revenge and further bloodshed between the two families, clans, or tribes. This practice is not very different from selling sheep or cattle as there are reports in the media that in some eastern regions of the country women are sold in exchange for cash. Here, again, this practice is contrary to Islam.

Aside from polygamy, there is also the issue of arranged marriage, especially among the uneducated and in the countryside. Parents, especially the father, has the final say on who their sons and daughters can marry. Afghans tend to marry within their family and *qawm*. Occasionally, intra-family engagements take place between first cousins at an early age so that they are not married off to "outsiders" later on.

Arranged marriage has advantages and disadvantages. Since Afghans prefer marrying their close relatives, the bride and bridegroom often know each other very well rather than marrying a complete stranger. Another positive aspect of arranged marriage is that a husband is hesitant to mistreat his cousin compared to someone to whom he is unrelated. Finally, in a society where minors get married, it is felt that it is better for the parents to do the selection for them because minors are not mature enough to make wise decisions.

One disadvantage of arranged marriage involving close cousins, however, is the perpetuation of hereditary defects. A more serious disadvantage of arranged marriage is that it amounts to forced marriage. According to a report put out by the British Womankind Worldwide in 2006, "Sixty to 80 percent of all marriages in Afghanistan are forced."[60] Some parents may ask their children for their opinion but the majority of parents do not. And when parents do ask their children for their opinion, it is usually the boy they talk to, not the girl. During the marriage ceremony, the mullah does not ask the bride directly if she accepts the bridegroom as her husband. Rather, it is the bride's representative (*wakil*) who speaks for her. Her representative rarely asks the girl for her opinion before talking to the cleric during the marriage license ceremony. In fact, this question and answer is only a ceremonial formality, as the answers from the bride and bridegroom are almost always positive. During the engagement ceremony, too, someone from the girl's family represents her and agrees to the engagement. It is the father who makes the final decision rather than the daughter.

Opposition to arranged marriage is rare in the country. Young couples who decide to marry without their parents' approval and run away to another town or city are eventually caught and put in jail. Unhappiness with marriage increases domestic violence and domestic violence in turn can lead to suicide by immolation on the part of wives. "Despite considerable progress following the collapse of the Taliban regime in 2001," says an international human rights organization, "self-immolations, forced marriages and rape remain widespread in Afghanistan."[61] Self-immolation is on the rise in Afghanistan, according to Medica Mondiala, a German-based NGO (nongovernmental organization) in Kabul. It says, "Hospitals in Kabul have treated 36 cases of self-immolation [in 2006] compared to 18 cases in 2005."[62] Cases of self-immolation have also been reported in Herat and Kandahar.

Domestic violence and the mistreatment of women are widespread in the country even though Islam emphasizes proper treatment of wives. The Qur'an says, "Live with them in kindness; even if you dislike them, perhaps you dislike something in which Allah has placed much good" (4:19). The Qur'an also says, "They [wives] are garments for you while you are garments for them" (2:187). "The best among you," goes a prophetic saying, "are those who are kindest to their wives."[63] Nonetheless, in practice, many Afghans mistreat their wives. Disobedient wives are punished verbally and physically. On dealing with a disobedient wife, the Qur'an says, "Council and admonish her first. If that does not help, then stay away from her bed; beat her up as a last resort."[64]

Marriage age is also a problem in Afghanistan, according to the United Nations statistics: "Although the legal marriage age is 18, 57 percent of girls are married before 16."[65] There are several reasons. One is that many parents, especially mothers, want to have grandchildren during their lifetime. Thus, to them, the sooner she marries the better. Another is that parents want to see their daughters "meet their fortune" (*pusht-e bakht-e khud bora*) as soon as possible and furthermore, "daughters are headaches" because they need so much watching over. This may be the reason for engaging female children to nephews as young as two, three, or four years old. Still another reason is that the majority of Afghan girls have no access to school so instead of being idle at home, it is better for them to get married. And finally, parents marry off their daughters at a very young age for economic reasons: poor families cannot feed their children and marrying a daughter off brings cash in the form of dowry or bride-price aside from providing for one less mouth to feed.

Aside from marriage, there is the contentious issue of divorce in Islam, which limits the rights of women. Islam encourages reconciliation and says divorce should be used only as a last resort. The Qur'an says, "And if you fear a breach between the two, then appoint a judge from his people and a judge from her people; if they both desire agreement, Allah will effect harmony between them, surely Allah is Knowing, Aware" (4:35).[66] A prophetic saying states that "Of all the things Allah has permitted, the one He most dislikes is divorce."[67] Divorce is also looked down on in the Afghan culture because among other things, a divorced person, especially a divorcee, has a hard time remarrying. This is why, as the saying goes, "A wife is like a mosque's door," implying that you cannot burn or destroy it because it is sacred. Consequently, many Afghan couples put up with their married lives. This is especially hard on women because men can take another wife if they are unhappy without divorcing the first. However, when divorce does occur it is usually the husband's prerogative. Even if the wife goes to court and asks for a divorce it is a long process and the husband usually wins the battle if he contests it.

Still another problematic issue involves inheritance. In Islam, males get more than women. Sons get twice as much as daughters and the widow, one-eighth of what is left from the father. The reason is that the responsibility of providing for the family is with men; women are not required to provide for the family. Therefore, men get more inheritance than women.

It is not just in inheritance that men get twice as much as women. In courts, too, for one male witness females must produce two. This, too, has its religious roots. Women are said to be more emotional than logical. To make up for this, the logic goes, there must be two women witnesses for every male witness. Obviously, this is contrary to human rights and other international laws.

Education

On education, Islam is clearly in favor of the education of both sexes. Here, too, the Qur'an and hadiths ("Traditions of the Prophet") emphasize *knowledge*: "seeking knowledge is the duty of every Muslim," "Seek knowledge even if it is in China," "A father who educates his daughter goes to Paradise," "When a mother is educated then a whole people are educated." In practice, however, the situation is very different. The education of males has priority over the education of females in Afghanistan. Only about six million children attend school, almost half of all Afghan children are not in school, and most of those enrolled are boys as only 1.6 million of them are girls. Female illiteracy is at least 90 percent.

Even if education is provided, religious training is more emphasized than secular. In fact, to the religious extremists, education of women is not necessary. That is why the Taliban closed all the schools for girls and banned their employment outside the home. Even in the schools for boys, religious education was emphasized. More *madrassas* (religious schools) mushroomed during the Taliban rule at the cost of secular schools for boys. Some human rights organizations refer to this dark period in Afghanistan as Women's Apartheid.

School curricula in the secular schools are also biased against women. History books are full of the achievements and bravery of men. There is very little, if any, mention of females; and what is said about women is always in connection with men. The religious textbooks teach *shari'a* (Islamic law) and Islamic history. The language arts textbooks, too, emphasize male domination through such themes as bravery, patriotism, sacrifice, and the struggle of men in society. During the Soviet occupation, the school textbooks in the regions under the Mujahideen control and in the refugee camps in Pakistan and Iran also emphasized jihadism (holy wars) and Islamist ideology. It is very likely that new school textbooks even today would do the same since the Mujahideen, including the current minister of education, Hanif Atmar, are dominating the government of Hamid Karzai.

Aside from the curriculum, teachers—most of whom are males—convey their bias against women to the students. Also, there are twice as many schools for boys as for girls. And in Kabul and other major cities, female teachers are not allowed to teach in boys' schools, but elderly religious teachers can teach Islamic studies in the schools for girls. Coeducation in Afghanistan is only at college and university level. And the situation of women is no better in employment either.

Employment

In Islam, both men and women have a role to play, but their role is based on their perceived nature. Women are perceived to be kind and affectionate by nature and men rational and logical. Therefore, according to Islamic jurisprudence, certain occupations require that affection and feelings be kept separate from logic and reasoning. For example, only men are suitable to be rulers, governors, judges, and jihadists. Women are not. This is consistent with early Islam when all the caliphs, judges, and commanders were men, and mostly males participated in the jihads or holy wars. Nowadays, too, in societies where Islamists rule, these occupations are not given to women. This was the case, for example, when the Mujahideen and Taliban were in power in Afghanistan. This situation also existed when the ulema (religious scholars) had strong influence in the government, for example, as was the case when Mohammed Nadir Khan was in power in the country in the early 1930s.

Due to the perceived nature of their nurturance, Afghan women traditionally have engaged primarily in teaching, medicine, nursing, and other health services. It is a characteristic of high MAS societies such as Afghanistan to consider some occupations typically male and others typically female.

The military, agriculture, mining, and other professions requiring physical work are off limits for women. However, women now have some professional jobs open to them. For the first time in the history of modern Afghanistan, Hamid Karzai has appointed a woman, Habiba Sarabi, as governor of Bamiyan. Some women are even now ministers in the present cabinet, though not for the first time. But these posts are given to women more for show and to satisfy the international community. Also for the first time in Afghan history, 25 percent of the parliamentarians are women due mostly to international pressure. And finally, for the first time, 1 percent of the judges in Afghanistan are women. However, since most of these improvements are due to the influence of the international community, attempts must be made to make these changes part of the social system so women will continue enjoying these roles even after pressure from the international community is long gone.

Women are also now employed in banks and ministries where they do office work. However, with a few exceptions, women are generally barred from many professions, including commerce and trade, and the Afghan Army. During the Communist governments, women were not only in the police and security but also in the army. Currently, there are women in the police force and security organizations in the country. If trained and given the opportunity, women would do just as well as men, if not better, in these and other careers held by men. According to the BBC Persian Web site, a woman has opened a shop in Mazar-e Sharif for the first time in the history of modern Afghanistan. It is the family that sets sex roles in education, employment, and others in society.

The Family

In the extended family of Afghan culture, the father is the absolute ruler. He makes the important decisions in marriage, career, travel, relationships, expenditures, and other family issues. Decision making is usually autocratic which must be obeyed by all members of the family. In fact, in some families, children refer to their father as *agha* (master). Disobedience is punished verbally, physically, and in every way possible depending on its nature and seriousness. In the absence of the father, the eldest son—not the eldest daughter or the mother—is usually the dominant figure in the family. But when there are no sons old enough to take the responsibility, the wife makes decisions; on more serious issues, the father's brother is consulted.

Children, male or female, learn to shoulder adult responsibilities at an early age. Female children participate in cooking, cleaning, doing the laundry, and other chores performed by the mother. Boys do work usually assigned to the father or another adult male in the family. For example, in the absence of his father, a ten- or twelve-year-old boy entertains unrelated male guests in the guest room by serving tea and or meals and talking to them. That is why a boy or a girl of twelve years of age in Afghanistan seems a lot more mature than children of the same age in the West. This "early maturity," however, comes with a price: the childhood period for Afghans is short, lasting no more than their first four or five years of life.

Division of labor in the family is based on sex. Males in the family usually do the work and chores outdoors and females indoors. In the countryside, females also work on the farm and fetch water for the family. Males, for example, never engage in cooking, washing, or cleaning unless there are no females in the house as it is considered "shameful" or "sissy" to play the role of a woman. When I came to America for the first time, I did not even know how to make eggs. I had to learn how to cook, not just eggs but also rice, soup, and other dishes. This is why sex roles are a problem for some Afghan immigrants in the United States. Wives want their husbands to clean and cook just as anyone else in America, but some husbands refuse and say such chores are a woman's responsibility.

There was an interesting satire related to this very issue in *Omaid*, a Dari weekly newspaper published in the United States. In the March 2007 issue, there was an interesting satire in which a married couple living in the

United States gets into an argument. The reason for the argument was that when the wife comes home from work she notices some unwashed dishes left from lunch. She tells her husband that he should have washed them as he does not work and he was home all day. The husband gets mad and says washing dishes is not *his* job. It is *her* job. She insists that both should do the household chores. The husband says that what he does at home—watching the news, reading and writing articles—is much more important than washing dishes. The argument gradually gets heated and becomes violent, and the husband beats his wife up. What is ironic in this satire is the fact that the husband was writing an article on the equality of men and women. The important message of this satire is that no matter how educated Afghan men are, they usually want to maintain their domination over women even if they live in a society where men and women are equal.

Aside from the household chores of cooking, cleaning, sewing, and so on, the mother and other female members of the family are also involved in teaching morality and ethics to the young children from an early age. Teaching children what to recite and how to pray is usually the mother's and other adult female's responsibility. In the countryside and some large towns, female children between the age of four and eight are sent to the mosque for religious training. Children, male or female, begin praying as early as seven or eight. Boys may go to the local mosque and girls pray at home. One of the changes I noticed during my trip to Afghanistan in 2002 was this rise of religiosity not just in small towns and villages but also in big cities such as Kabul. This was quite different from the time I was living in Kabul twenty-three years ago when it was mostly adults who prayed on a regular basis.

In terms of marriage, children—male and female— usually wait their turn. Older children get married first.

Since male children are more important and the marriage of females in the family does not cost any money, the entire family keeps its savings for the marriage of the male members. If there are, for example, two sons, they both give their income to the father to save for their marriage. Once the elder son gets married, the family begins to save for the marriage of the second son, and so on. The females, too, get married based on their age. If a family, for example, has two daughters and a suitor wants the younger one for a bride, he or she is told the younger is not "ready." Again, Islam does not order Muslims to have lavish weddings; the custom is based on the attitude that women can be bought or sold like chattel Islam is opposed to sibling inequality. It encourages the father to treat all members of the family the same. "The Qur'an says that God has created men and women from the same water and mud (*nafs-e wahid*)."[68] The Prophet Mohammad says, "Whoever has a son and a daughter and does not favor the son over the daughter goes to heaven."[69] Thus, sibling inequality is more due to male domination and superiority in the Afghan culture than to Islam.

Nonetheless, boys get royal treatment in the family. Boys are the favorite for several reasons. One is that the birth of a son in the family is potentially an additional family income down the road. Islam gives only men the responsibility of providing for the family, not women. With the exception of female carpet weavers in the north of the country, women generally do not make any money and very few seek employment outside of the home. Another reason why sons are preferred over daughters in Afghanistan is that the former, aside from performing work requiring physical strength, defend the family in case a fight breaks out between two families, related or unrelated. In the absence of the rule of law, a family with more sons feels more secure in the neighborhood; there is no 911 to call, and the police do not exist in the countryside. Even in the towns and cities, they arrive too late. Finally, and perhaps most importantly, a son stays with the family and, as the saying goes, "He keeps the name of the father alive." In Afghanistan, especially among the Pashtun, one's genealogy is traced through the father's side, not that of the mother. A daughter, on the other hand, is said to be "other people's property" because she eventually gets married and leaves the family. This is why Afghans are proud of their sons and love to talk about them but not about their daughters, especially to distant relatives and strangers. Thus, in greetings, they ask about the health of the male members but omit the females completely.

The father and the other adult males always keep an eye on the females in the family, making sure they have no contact with males outside of the extended family, either inside the family compound or outside. In small towns and villages, when traveling, a female is always accompanied by a male member of the family called *mahram* (a person with whom marriage is *haram*, or prohibited) regardless of whether the trip is short or long, inside the village or town, or outside, she must be accompanied at all times outside the house.

Prior to the civil war, in large cities and towns, very few women were accompanied when traveling. However, during the Taliban period, checking the presence or absence of a *haram* accompanying a female was made one of the responsibilities of a newly established ministry. This policy even continued during the reign of Hamid Karzai. For example, according to a Human Rights Watch report put out in 2002, when Ismail Khan was the governor of Herat, women seen alone in a taxi or walking on the street with a male would be taken to a hospital for gynecological examination to determine if sexual intercourse had recently taken place.

Dating is absolutely prohibited in Afghanistan. Violators of this unwritten rule are severely punished including death. In 2004, for example, one of my relatives, "Sanjed"[70] killed his sister "Zayba" for "talking" to a boy, "Ahmad," in their neighborhood in Chilsotoon, south of Kabul City. Sanjed asked his mother to get something from the store. Then he took Zayba to the storage room and suffocated her with her scarf. Sanjed then escaped but a couple of months later was arrested. Police investigations showed that Sanjed had planned to kill Ahmad as well. Even in the West, where dating is part of the culture, first generation Afghans do everything they can to prevent their children from dating and getting married on their own. In 2006 in Sweden, for example, a Pashtun Afghan girl, "Samira" after dating a Hazara boy, "Ali" decided to get married but their parents, especially Samira's, opposed the marriage. Samira and Ali decided to run away from their families. Later, when Samira called home, her father "Jalal" told her that he had changed his mind and he was now ready to arrange their wedding. The two of them then came to Samira's home. Upon their arrival, though, Jalal and his son tied Ali's hands and poured boiling cooking oil on his face and killed him. It was not clear what the parents did to the girl. Thus, dating even by the second generation remains a problem for the first generation Afghan immigrants in North America and other Western countries which can sometimes end in a tragedy.

In Afghan culture, women are treated as property. In some parts of the country, women are sold as cattle. One of Khaled Hosseini's characters in his recent novel, *A Thousand Splendid Suns* compares his wives with cars, calling the one he likes a Mercedes Benz and the one he dislikes a Russian Volga. It is worth noting in this connection that this novel gives an excellent portrayal of life for Afghan women in society.

Since women are treated as property, a stranger's talking to, looking at or touching a woman is taboo in the Afghan national culture. That is why most Afghan women do not want to shake hands with a stranger, especially a non-Muslim. It is worse than trespassing in individualistic societies such as the United States. Thus, unless a woman extends her hand first, a stranger should not shake hands with women.

Afghan women wear the Islamic *hijab* (cover). The *hijab* can be a scarf (*chadar*) or a head-to-toe garment, shaped like an upside down lettuce called *chadari* or *burqa*. Prior to the civil war, the chadari was worn by women mostly in the countryside; but in large cities and towns, educated women wore the *chadar*. Nowadays, however, thanks to the Taliban's imposition of a strict code of clothing, even in Kabul more women wear the *chadari* while a small number wear the *chadar*. The change apparently is due to an increase in religiosity and/or a measure, on the part of young and single girls, against potential kidnapping and forced marriage. It is worth noting that the color of the *chadari* depends on the age of the woman, education, and other factors. Older women prefer white or gray, for example.

Usually, family members eat all the meals together. In large extended families, men and women eat separately, with men eating first. In weddings and other social gatherings, too, men and women usually sit in separate rooms, and they are fed separately with men being served first. In Kabul and other large cities however, weddings take place at restaurants where men and women may sit together and everyone is fed at one time.

In Afghan culture, the family and *qawm* are responsible for the behavior of their members just as members are responsible to them. This is why when a family member commits a crime and runs away, the authorities force his family to find him.

Afghan Human Rights Activists

In addition to international human rights organizations such as Human Rights Watch, Womankind Worldwide, Amnesty International, and others involved in women's rights in Afghanistan, there are also Afghan female intellectuals as well as an Afghan human rights organization in the country. Among the activist female intellectuals, some are well-known such as Dr. Sima Samar, head of the Afghan Independent Human Rights Commission in Kabul and Malalai Joya, a member of the Afghan Parliament. Both Samar and Joya attacked the Mujahideen openly in the Loya Jirga (grand assembly). Afghan intellectuals admire and respect their courage. Although 25 percent of the current parliament are women, only a small number of them, such Ms. Joya and a few other female politicians speak up for women's rights in Afghanistan. The primary reason is that female activists such as Samar and Joya have been targets of intimidation and even violence.

Aside from a small number of female activists, there is also an active organization supporting women's rights called RAWA (the Revolutionary Association of the Women of Afghanistan). This organization was founded in Kabul in 1977, "as an independent political organization fighting for human rights and for social justice in Afghanistan . . . [it] advocates democracy and secularism."[71] It has a magazine, *Payam-e-Zan* (the Message of Women) with articles in both Dari and Pashto "to give Afghan women social and political awareness in regard to their rights."[72] In the view of some Mujahideen, these female activists are also members of RAWA.

RAWA was very active during the occupation of Afghanistan by the former Soviet Union. Its involvement during this period was mostly in providing health and other social services to Afghan women in the refugee camps, mostly in Quita, Pakistan, and in Iran. This organization publicized rapes, killings, kidnappings, and other atrocities committed against women in Afghanistan during the reign of the Mujahideen and the Taliban. Perhaps RAWA's most important contribution has been its publicizing of the Taliban's atrocities against Afghan women to the outside world. RAWA's videos of the Taliban's public executions and stoning of Afghan women shown on Western television stations turned the U.S. public, especially women, against the Taliban movement, forcing the U.S. government not to recognize it. At the time (1992-1993), the United States had been considering officially recognizing the Taliban regime, following Pakistan and some of the countries in the Persian Gulf. Denial of recognition of the Taliban regime on the part of the United States made the movement become more anti-American, giving Osama bin-Ladin's al-Qaeda a free hand to intensify its terrorist activities which eventually led to the 9/11 attacks in New York and Washington in 2001. This in turn resulted in the overthrow of the Taliban by the United States.

MAS in the Workplace

In addition to some of the tips provided in the previous chapters, a female Westerner should try to be extra careful in the workplace. Since Afghans do not want to take orders from a woman, a female Westerner supervisor should come across as an authoritarian from the very first day. She needs to avoid joking and laughing, especially during the first two or three weeks. Smiling and being too friendly sends the wrong message. She should avoid wearing pants, dress conservatively, and behave very professionally. In short, she should be strictly businesslike and professional.

Afghans ask personal questions such as one's age, marital status, income, and so on. The best response to such questions might be to give evasive answers and change the subject to work-related matters.

What is important is professionalism and establishing authority. Initially, it will be hard to have a woman as their boss; but after a while, they will accept your authority. Here again, be fair and firm and avoid accepting dinner or lunch invitations until you get to know your staff. If there are females working for you, try to socialize with them a few minutes a day. If a female subordinate does something well, talk about it to the rest of the employees.

If the female Westerner is a coworker, she should also avoid joking and smiling with men. With female coworkers, it is different. Maintain your professionalism at all times. Both male and female Westerners should avoid discussing religion and politics, at least in the workplace. Westerners should try to learn the language even if it is only greetings and leave-takings. It shows you care about the people and the country you are in.

A male Westerner, coworker, or supervisor, should stay away from female Afghans in the workplace. Contact should be related to business only. A male coworker should socialize with men only and a female coworker with females.

As a supervisor, male or female, the Westerner should try to hire more women and encourage female subordinates more than the male ones. Discourage men from ridiculing or harassing women in the workplace.

Conclusions

Afghanistan is a male-dominated society where women are treated as property and whose primary function is procreation. Sex roles for men and women are fixed in the family; and they are reinforced in schools, employment, and other social organizations.

It is Islamic fundamentalism and Afghan cultural traditions rather than mainstream Islam that limit the rights of women in Afghanistan, making the country a high MAS culture. To the extremists, women are supposed to stay indoors and be at the service of men. "In Afghan cultural traditions, women are regarded as cattle, exchanged as compensation for a crime, or to settle a debt or to make profit-bride-price. Weak justice, illiteracy, and poverty are the primary cause of violence against women."[73] And finally, the primary purpose of marriage in societies with high MAS is reproduction rather than recreation.

Under the present circumstances, what Afghan women are most in need of is more economic support, security, and justice. One has to have enough to eat and to feel safe before thinking of equality and rights. For the first time in modern Afghan history, women are providing for their families. Reportedly, there are one million widows in the country struggling to support themselves and their children. They need education and training, and mini-bank loans to engage in small businesses, such as sewing and other handcrafts or raising chickens. Afghanistan needs to have its own Muhammad Yunus, the Nobel Peace Prize winner for 2006, who is a pioneer in making tiny loans to impoverished women and men and other credit-poor entrepreneurs in Bangladesh. At first, he made $27 loans from his own pocket. Now, however, he has his own bank, Grameen Bank, with ten thousand microfinance institutions holding more than seven billion dollars in outstanding loans. Afghan women, especially widows, would benefit tremendously from such a microfinance system to help them establish such small businesses.

The media, too, needs to launch a campaign to improve the sad situation of women, especially the widows. For example, both victims and victimizers should be interviewed and their names and pictures made public in the electronic and print media. The international community could fund the training and education of women, especially widows. The 120,000 addicted women also need special attention.

The Afghan government must pay special attention to the safety of women. They should be protected against forced marriage, verbal and physical abuse. Here the role of both the security forces and the courts is crucial. Here, too, the ulema's contribution is very significant in improving the courts by increasing the number of female judges and imposing harsher punishment for abusers of women in domestic violence cases.

Food for Thought

(1) Why is it that getting engaged is such a long process in Afghanistan?

(2) What are the possible consequences of flirting with subordinates and coworkers?

(3) Prior to the civil war, some Afghan students in the United States married American girls and some American men working in Afghanistan married Afghan girls. There are no statistics, but my observations indicate that most of the marriages in the former category have not lasted long, whereas those in the second have. Why?

(4) As a Westerner, is it appropriate to attend a subordinate's invitation to come to his or her engagement party? Why?

(5) Why is that the government of Afghanistan is more supportive of men than women? What are the consequences of such a policy in employment and education?

(6) Why is it that the status of women in Afghanistan was a lot better, prior to the civil war?

(7) Why are there so few female activists in Afghanistan?

(8) Why is it that the majority of Afghan women are hesitant to join the ANA or ANP?

(9) Is it appropriate to use the same criteria in hiring men and women? Why?

(10) What should be the role of the international community in improving the status of women in Afghanistan? Should foreign assistance be conditional on the improvement of the condition of women in Afghanistan? Why, or why not?

(11) As far as polygamy is concerned, what are some similarities between the Mormons in the United States and the Afghans?

CHAPTER 5

Summary and Conclusions

Power distance, the first dimension of culture, refers to the relationship between a strong individual and a weak one, such as the president to a citizen, a supervisor to a subordinate, a commander to a soldier, a teacher to a student, a father to a family, and so on. There are degrees of power distance between national cultures: some are high and others are low. Afghanistan is a high power distance society, whereas the United State, for example, is a low one.

Some cultural traits that correlate with power distance in Afghan culture are social power, power and wealth, expert power, decision-making norms, elitism and pluralism, age and charisma, and the authority of the person (the authority of the individual or person and not the position, i.e., president or king.) Social power is coercive in the Afghan national culture but democratic in the American national culture. Afghan rulers have come to power by force, stayed in power by force, and were ousted by force. During the last 120 years, some Afghan rulers have been murdered (Habibullah Khan, Habibullah Kalakani, Nadir Khan, Daoud Khan, Nur Muhammad Taraki, Hafizullah Amin, and Dr. Najibullah) while others ousted and still alive (Sebghatullah Mujaddidi, Burhanudin Rabbani, and Mullah Omar).

In Afghanistan, it is the authority of the person that carries weight, not the authority of the rule or position. This is true of families, organizations, and the country as a whole. Throughout the history of Afghanistan, weak rulers who have not been able to maintain law and order have not stayed in power for long.

Power and wealth are inseparable in Afghan society. Power brings wealth, and wealth makes one powerful. Once in power, Afghans tend to fill their pockets and accumulate wealth as soon as possible through legal and illegal means. This is especially the case when the country is not so stable and a great deal of foreign funds are available. This explains the high degree of corruption in Afghanistan today. It is said that about 40 percent of foreign donations and assistance is misdirected. With wealth, one can get to a position of power in the government. In low power distance societies such as America, on the other hand, power and wealth are separable; one can be wealthy but not powerful in such societies.

In high power distance societies such as Afghanistan, knowledge as expert power is not valued so much. Who you know (*rawabit*, connections) rather than *what* you know (*zawabit*, principles)" is what counts. This is the primary reason for the brain drain in the developing societies. Decision making is autocratic and consultative in Afghanistan rather than persuasive and democratic. Hence, Afghans rely on assemblies (*jirgahs*) and councils (*shuras*), both in public and private.

Afghan society is elitist rather than pluralistic. The elite dominate the three branches of the government and run the affairs of the country. The new elites in Afghanistan are mostly the former Mujahideen leaders and commanders, and Western-educated technocrats. Finally, in a high power distance national culture, age and charisma play a crucial role.

High power distance in the Afghan national culture has implications for disarmament, narcotics, democratization, reconstruction, leadership and employment, peace and security, as well as terrorism in the country.

Uncertainty avoidance, the second dimension of culture, involves how societies deal with fear from nature, other men, and the supernatural. The criteria used to determine the degree of uncertainty avoidance in societies are stress, job stability, and rule orientation. Some cultures are on the low side of uncertainty avoidance and others on the high side. In high uncertainty avoidance societies such as Afghanistan, there is less tolerance for uncertainty and ambiguity whereas in low uncertainty avoidance societies such as the United States, there is more tolerance of uncertainty.

The three methods used in coping with uncertainty are laws, technology, and religion. Technology involves all the artifacts man has created to defend itself against nature, laws are the rules and rituals used to deal with fear from other men, and religion is used to lessen fear of the supernatural. Generally, modern nations such as the United States make more use of technology and law to reduce uncertainty, whereas traditional ones such as Afghanistan rely on religion to deal with uncertainty.

Some consequences of being on the high side of uncertainty avoidance include the political system, dependence on experts, seniority and theory. Politically, citizen competence in Afghanistan is low in that people cannot protest the decisions made and, thus, feel helpless in changing the political system. In low uncertainty avoidance societies such as the United States, citizen competence involves participation in local and national politics and protests against decisions.

Afghanistan also shares some of the emphasis high uncertainty avoidance societies place on theory rather than on practice. For example, Afghan higher education stresses theoretical knowledge more than its practical applications. This is in sharp contrast to the community colleges in the United States, which serve the practical needs of the communities. And at the American university level, practical applications of knowledge are emphasized. It is the emphasis on empiricism that explains why so many of the Nobel Prize winners come from the United States.

Dependence on experts is still another characteristic of high uncertainty-avoiding countries. There is so much emphasis on expert knowledge in these cultures that even managerial jobs are performed by experts. For example, the minister of health, a managerial position, has almost always been a medical doctor. It has been the same with the ministry of defense and other ministries. In low avoidance societies such as the United States, on the other hand, such positions are held by people with expertise in managing. The secretary of defense, for instance, has been a civilian with no specialized education expertise in military affairs. This is based on the belief that certain tasks can be performed by laymen with managerial skills.

Finally, seniority is still another trait of high uncertainty-avoiding societies such as Afghanistan. Unlike the United States, in Afghanistan older people do not allow younger people to take decision making in their hands. For the same reason, Afghans do not trust leaders younger than fifty years of age. In short, there is gerontocracy or rule of the old in Afghanistan.

Since there is not much technology or the rule of law in Afghanistan, Islam is the primary defense not just against nature and other men but also to lessen fear from the supernatural. Religious attitudes with regard to uncertainty avoidance are based on three fundamental beliefs. One is that life in this world is temporary and what is truly permanent is life after death. The second fundamental belief is that God is the source of both good and evil. Finally, God is just and will punish the oppressors in this world and the next. These beliefs provide the Afghans with a mechanism to cope with the hardship and uncertainties of their lives.

The third dimension of culture involves individualism versus collectivism, the relationship of an individual to a group or collectivity. Some societies such as Afghanistan are collectivistic, whereas others, such as the United States, are individualistic. In collectivistic societies, the individual is at the service of the group or other collectivity; and in return, the group protects the individual. A collectivity such as the family usually makes important decisions such as marriage, education, and others for the individual. In general, high power distance countries are more collectivistic and low power distance ones more individualistic.

Afghanistan shares some of the characteristics of the collectivistic cultures: low economic development, less social mobility, weak development of the middle class, less dependence on individual initiative, more traditional agriculture, less modern industry, more emphasis on extended family, tribalism, more children in the nuclear family, more traditional education and religious education, more collectivistic thinking and action, less press freedom, more political repression, and potential policies and practices based on relations and ties.

Ingroup loyalties are reflected in Afghan nationalism. Nationalism does not have the same meaning in the West and in the East. In societies such as Afghanistan, one is first loyal to his or her family, tribe, and other collectivity and only after to the country as a whole. In other words, in Afghanistan, one is first a Pashtun, a Tajik, a Hazara, and so on and then an Afghan. This is characteristic of non-nation-states. In nation-states such as the United States, one's loyalties lie with the state rather than the family, ethnic group, or any other group or collectivity. In the absence of the rule of law and democracy, Afghan nationalism is the only mechanism for survival.

The dimensions of Afghan nationalism are ethnicity (race and language), sect (Sunni or Shi'a), regionalism (place of birth), and ideology. Of these dimensions, ethnicity has been the most dangerous throughout the history of modern Afghanistan. Language and race have always been and still are sensitive issues in Afghanistan. Among the ethnic groups, the Pashtuns have been mostly in power since Afghanistan was founded in 1747. That is why Pastuns have engaged in bloody battles with the Hazaras and the Tajiks. The most recent ethnic conflicts took place between the Pashtun Taliban and the non-Pashtun Tajiks and Hazaras during the recent civil war in Afghanistan.

The concept of a nation-state is a Western phenomenon. After World War I in 1923, Turkey was the first Muslim country to make this concept a reality. Other Islamic countries tried to follow suit. Afghanistan tried to become a nation-state too, but it failed. That is why the country is not and has never been a nation-state. In a nation-state, there is rule of law, democracy, separation of church and state, checks and balances, freedom of the press, political parties, and free and fair elections.

An important step in the direction of making Afghanistan a nation-state may be some type of Federalism, as the conditions for a strong centralized government no longer exist due to the geopolitical and societal changes.

The fourth dimension culture is masculinity (MAS) or the gender gap involving the equality or lack thereof between men and women in societies. Just as in the other dimensions of culture, there are degrees of MAS. Some societies are on the high side and others are in the middle or the low side. MAS is high in Afghanistan but low in the United

States and other Western democracies. MAS correlates positively with power distance and uncertainty avoidance but negatively with individualism.

Masculinity is associated with assertiveness and femininity with nurturance. Assertiveness in the workplace is associated with management, leadership, advancement, power, earnings, recognition, independence, endurance, loyalty, among others. Nurturance, on the other hand, involves patience, obedience, emotion, yielding, submission, and tenderness. In general, men are more assertive and women more nurturing.

Sex roles are determined by cultural norms in society. They are learned early in life in the family and are reinforced in school and other organizations in a culture. Sex roles and attitudes toward women in Afghanistan are reflected in the language and literature, religion, educational system, employment, and the family.

There are some national and international organizations and female activists involved in improving the status of Afghan women in the country. On the national level, there is the Afghan Human Rights and RAWA. On the international level, there are the Womankind Worldwide and Human Rights Watch. The well-known Afghan female activists include Dr. Sima Samar, head of the Afghan Human Rights and Malalai Joya, member of the Afghan Parliament.

To meet the immediate and long-term needs of Afghan women, the book makes some recommendations to the Afghan government, the ulema (religious scholars), the general public, the media, and the international community. The urgent and immediate needs of Afghan women, especially the widows and the drug-addicted females, are economic support and security. In the longer term, Afghan women need access to more education and employment. Domestic violence is on the rise in

Afghanistan and the lives of female journalists and others are threatened. For example, on June 6, 2007, Mrs. Zakia Zaki, who was in charge of Radio Peace in Jabul saraj, Parwan province, was murdered in her house by intruders. This was after Shekaiba Sanga, another female working for Shamshad Television, had been murdered at her house in Kabul on May 31, 2007.

It is important to note that these dimensions are interrelated. For example, being on the high side power distance, Afghan national culture is also on the high side of uncertainty avoidance and masculinity but on the low side of individualism while at the same time has short-term orientation. This in turn shapes the worldview and how they think and behave. Also, cultural traits can be explained by more than dimension. For example, holding councils are parts of both power distance and collectivism. Finally, the roots of most of these dimensions are the family where cultural norms are set.

BIBLIOGRAPHY

The sources consulted for this study

Abdu-Rahman, Amir. *Tjutawarikh.* vols. 1 and 2. Peshawar, Pakistan: Maywand Publications, 1985.

Abraishumi, Ahmad. *Farhang-e Naween-e Guzida-ye Masalha-ye Farsi* (New Selected Dictionary of Farsi Proverbs). Tehran: Zewar Publishers, 1988.

Ahmadi Khurasani, Nooshin, ed. *Gens-e Dowom: A Collection of Articles.* n.p.: Tehran, Iran. 1997

Ansari, Khwaja Bashirahmad. "The Yakawlang Bleeding Wound." *Omaid Weekly.* February 5, 2007, p. 5. No. 772.

Badawi, Jamal A. *Gender Equity in Islam: Basic Principles.* Indiana: American Trust Publications, 1995.

Bonner, Arthur. *Among the Aghans.* Durham and London: Duke University Press, 1987.

Dupree, Louis. *Afghanistan.* Princeton, NJ: Princeton University Press, 1973.

Entezar, Ehsan "*Afghanistan-e Naween Wa Moazal-ye wahdat-e milee*" (The New Afghanistan and the Problem of

National Unity). Serialized in *Omaid Weekly*. Virginia, USA, January 2002.

Friedl, Erika. *Women of Deh Koh*. New York: Penguin Books, 1989.

Ghubar, Ghulam Muhammad. *Afghanistan dar Maseer-e Tarikh* (Afghanistan in the Course of History), Markaz-e Enqilab, [Iran?]: 1986.

_____. *Afghanistan dar Masser-e Tarikh* (Afghanistan in the Course of History) Vol. 2. Virginia, USA, 1999.

Hofstede, Geert. *Culture's Consequences: International Differences in Work-related Values*. Newbury Park, CA: Sage Publications, 1980.

_____. *Culture and Organizations: Software of the Mind*. New York: McGrawhill, January 2005.

Hosseini, Khaled. *The Kite Runner*, New York: Riverhead Books, 2003.

_____. A Thousand Splendid Suns, New York: Riverhead Books, 2006.

Kohn, Hans. *The Age of Nationalism*. New York: Harper and Row, 1962.

Maley, William, *The Afghanistan Wars*. New York: Palgrave Macmillan, 2002.

McChesney, Robert D. *Kabul under Siege: Faiz Muhammad's Account of the 1929 Uprising*. 1999.

Mir-Hosseini, Ziba. *Marriage on Trial: A Study of Islamic Family Law*. New York: I. B. Tauris & Co. Ltd. Publishers, London, 1993.

Mousavi, Sayed Askar. *The Hazaras of Afghanistan: A Historical, Cultural, and Political Study*. Curzan Press, 1998.

Poladi, Hassan. *The Hazaras*. Stockton, California: Mughal Publishing Co., 1989.

Shahrani, Nazif M. and Canfield, Robert L. *Revolution & Rebellions in Afghanistan: Anthropological Perspectives. Burkley: Institute of International Studies*, 1984.

Rafugaran, Farayba. "A Look at the Definition of Man and Woman in the Dehkhuda Dictionary," in *The Second Sex*. Edited by Nushin Ahmadi Khurasani. Tehran: n.p., 1979.

Roy, Olivier. Edited by Myron Weiner and Ali Banuazizi. "The New Political Elites of Afghanistan." *The Politics of Social Transformation in Afghanistan, Iran, and Pakistan*. Syracuse: Syracuse University Press, 1994.

Satari, Jalal. *Seema-ye Zzan dar Farhang-eIran* (Image of Woman in Iranian Society). Tehran, Iran: Sadi Printing Press, 1994.

Stewart, Rory. *The Places in Between*, Orlando: Harcourt, Inc., 2004.

Stewart, Rory, *The Places in Between*. A Harvest Original. Orlando: Harcourt, Inc., 2004.

Weiner, Myron and Banuazizi, Ali. Eds. *The Politics of Social Transformation in Afghanistan, Iran, and Pakistan.* Syracuse, New York: Syracuse University Press, 1994.

APPENDIX:
AFGHAN ETHNIC
GROUPS

Afghanistan is a mosaic of ethnic groups due to the invasions of the Greeks, Arabs, Mongols, Turks over the centuries. The Afghan ethnic groups include the Pashtuns, Tajiks, Hazaras, Uzbeks, Aimaqs, Baluchis, Pashayees, Turkmens, Nuristanis, and others. The first four are the major ones.

The Pashtuns

The largest ethnic group (40 percent) in the country is the Pashtun. They refer to themselves as *Pashtana* or *Pukhtana* (Pashtuns), but the non-Pashtuns refer to them as *Afghan/Awghans* (Afghans). A Pashtun is one who speaks Pashto natively and adheres to orthodox Sunni Islam. They are concentrated in the south and east of Afghanistan.

Like Dari, Pashto belongs to the Indo-Iranian branch of the Indo-European family of languages, and the Pashtuns are basically a Mediterranean form of the Caucasian race or Aryan (Iranian). In addition to Afghanistan, Pashto is also spoken in the northwestern frontier province of Pakistan. That is why the Pashtun tribes in eastern Afghanistan have close kin in Pakistan. Pashto dialects differ in

pronunciation and vocabulary. The two major dialects of
Pashto in the country are "Pashto" and "Pukhto." The
former is dialect of the southwest (Kandahar, Helmand,
Oruzgan) and the latter that of the eastern regions. Thus,
from the pronunciation, one can tell where a Pashtun
is from. For example, the word for *mister* is pronounced
shaghilay (Pashto dialect) in Kandahar, but *khaghilay*
(Pukhto dialect) in Paktia, Nangarhar, and other eastern
provinces of Afghanistan. Unlike the Afghan Pashtuns,
Pakistani Pashtuns use a lot of loan words from Urdu and
English and speak the language with an Urdu accent.
Pashto grammar is also much more complex than that of
Dari. For example, unlike Dari, it has both gender and
case. Due to the influence of Persian and Arabic, Pashto
has a lot of loan words and loan translations from these
two languages as well. Pashto is written with the Arabic
alphabet with added characters to accommodate for its own
consonants and vowels.

The Pashtun-dominated regimes have tried in vain to
make Pashto the lingua franca in Afghanistan. To this end,
in the late 1930s, government employees were required to
learn Pashto; and in the constitution of 1964, Pashto and
Dari were made the official language of Afghanistan, but
Pashto was the national language. Other "Pashtunization"
measures included the establishment of the Pashto
Society, making it at one time the language of instruction
in all primary and secondary schools and changing all the
signs into Pashto as well as other initiatives mentioned in
chapter three.

Of all the ethnic groups, the Pashtuns have the most
complex criteria of ethnic identity and code of honor.
Genealogy is more important among the Pashtuns than
the other ethnic groups in Afghanistan. The Pashtuns trace
their descent to Qais Abdur Rashid. In their mythology,
Pashtuns trace their ancestry to the ten lost tribes of Israel,

who, after their captivity in Babylon, ended up in Ghor, west of the Hazarajat in central Afghanistan.

Pashtuns are known for their code of honor, *pashtunwali*, a legal and moral code that determines social order and personal responsibilities. Pashtunwali includes values such as honor (*naamoos*), hospitality (*mailmustia*), solidarity (*nang*), compensation for blood (*badal*), bravery (*ghairat*), asylum (*nanawati*), and so on. It is worth noting that such a code of honor also exists among the other ethnic groups in Afghanistan in one form or another though not as strict and intensive as that of the Pashtuns. As has been pointed out in chapter 3, these legal and moral codes are necessary for survival in societies where there is no rule of law and democracy.

Like other ethnic groups in Afghanistan, Pashtuns in different regions, while sharing some common traditions and customs, have their own distinguishing characteristics. For example, one can tell where a Pashtun comes from on the basis of the color of his turban and how he ties it. Pashtuns living among the Tajiks and other non-Pashtun ethnic groups have adopted the local customs in clothing and other things. It is the Pashtuns who are bilinguals—learning Pashto at home and the local language from the environment. More specifically, these Pashtuns live in Kabul, Herat, and the northern provinces of Afghanistan.

Unlike the other ethnic groups, Pashtun culture is tribal, but its structure is not hierarchical. Individuals with high social status make up the leadership of a tribe. The two major Pashtun tribes in Afghanistan are the Durrani (lit. "pearl of the age") and the Ghilzai, each of which is divided into clans and subclans. Other Pashtun tribes include Wardak, Jaji, Mangal, Tanai, Zedran (Jedran), Shinwari, and Safi. The Durrani tribe, making up most of the Taliban, mostly come from the southwest—Kandhar,

Helmand, and Oruzgan—while the Ghilzais (Gilzais) are mostly located in the southeast and eastern part of the country.

Almost all of the monarchs and the ruling oligarchy of modern Afghanistan, including the current president, Hamid Karzai, come from the Durrani tribes. In fact, it was Ahmad Shah Durrani, also known as Ahmad Shah Abdali, who founded the country in 1747. Hence, the name Durrani. A few of the Ghilzais have also ruled Afghanistan. Mirwias Khan or Mirwais Baba ruled both Afghanistan and some parts of modern Iran prior to the founding of modern Afghanistan. In more recent times, the late presidents, Nur Muhammad Taraki and Hafizullah Amin, were also Ghilzais. There has been political rivalry between these tribes. It was the Ghilzais who toppled the Durrani government of President Mohammad Daoud in the Communist Coup 1978. In the Karzai government, almost all the Pashtuns holding key positions are Ghilzais.

The major Pashtun political groups, in addition to the Taliban, include *Afghan Milat* (Afghan Nation), led by Anwar ul-Haq Ahadi, a Ghilzai and the current minister of finance; *Itihad-e Islami Afghanistan* (Islamic Unity of Afghanistan), led by Rasul Sayyaf, a Ghilzai and member of parliament; and *Hizb-e Islami* (the Islamic Party), led by Gulbuddin Hekmatyar, another Ghilzai who has gone underground and is fighting the government and the coalition and ISAF/NATO forces in the country.

There is bad blood between the Pashtuns and other ethnic groups, especially the Tajiks and Hazaras. For example, when the Taliban came to power, most of the fighting took place with the non-Pashtuns, namely the Tajiks, Hazaras, and Uzbeks. It was mostly the Tajiks who resisted the Taliban and would not allow them to capture the entire country. The Taliban also fought several bloody battles with the Hazaras in Bamiyan and Balkh provinces before capturing these regions. Their hatred of the Hazaras is specially strong because most Hazaras are Shi'is. For the same reason, the Pashtuns do not like the Iranians, who are also Shi'is. As a result of the Taliban's animosity toward these two non-Pashtun ethnic groups, they launched their ethnic cleansing campaigns with an ultimate goal of eliminating all the minorities from Afghanistan. In *The Kite Runner*, Khaled Hosseini, the Afghan novelist, provides an excellent portrayal of how Hazaras are treated by the Pashtuns in Afghan society.

The majority of Pashtuns engage in farming. Some are traders and shopkeepers and others, such as the nomads (*kuchis*), are herdsmen. Since most of the poppy cultivation is in the southwest and east of Afghanistan, the majority of the poppy farmers, drug traffickers and smugglers are Pashtuns. Their ties to their fellow ethnic Pashtuns in Pakistan make it easier to smuggle drugs, arms, and other things in and out of the country.

The Tajiks

Tajiks are the second major ethnic group in Afghanistan. Known as Daygan among the Pashtuns, the Tajik make up about 27 percent of the population of the country. A Tajik is defined as a person who speaks Dari as his or her native language and adheres to the Sunni sect of Islam. Some Shi'i Afghans, known as the Qizelbash are of the same race as the Tajiks. They are Imamis or Ithna-Asharis (Twelvers) and are mostly concentrated in the capital Kabul in the districts of Chindawul and Afshar.

The word *Dari* is the official name for the language an average Afghan refers to as "Farsi." Dari, like Pashto, belongs to the Indo-Iranian branch of the Indo-European family of languages. The other Indo-Iranian language spoken in Afghanistan is Baluchi spoken by the Afghan,

Pakistani, and Iranian Baluches. Dari is one of three major dialects of Persian; the other two are Farsi, spoken in Iran and Tajiki/Tajik, spoken in Tajikistan and Uzbekistan, north of Afghanistan. These three dialects differ in pronunciation, vocabulary, and even syntax. Iranian Farsi has more French loan words and Tajiki more Russian. But they are mutually intelligible as, by definition, dialects are supposed to be. For a Westerner going to Afghanistan, it is better to learn Dari or Pashto depending on whether the assignment is in a Dari—or Pashto-speaking location. For example, going to Kandahar or any other city in the south one would be better off learning Pashto, but going to Kabul and other locations other than the south or east Dari would be the more appropriate language to learn.

Dari is the *lingua franca* or interethnic language of Afghanistan. That is why the majority of the other ethnic groups, especially those living in major towns and cities, also speak it as a second language. Dari has always been the language of the royal courts, business, and trade in Afghanistan. King Abdul Rahman Khan's scribe, for example, was a Hazara known as Sarkatib even though the king was a Pashtun. Court scribers, accountants, and poets were also Dari speakers. For example, Sultan Mahmmod, a Turk who ruled in the tenth century, had four hundred Persian poets in his court. Some famous scholars, writers, poets, and warriors were Tajiks. Avicenna and Rumi (also known as Mawlana) are examples. A more recent warrior and commander is the legendary Commander Ahmad Shah Massoud, known as the "Lion of Panjshir" who fought the Soviet occupiers and later the Taliban until the last drop of his blood. Of all the Mujahideen known commanders, he was the only one who stayed almost all of the time inside Afghanistan instead of fleeing to Tajikistan, Uzbekistan, Pakistan, Iran, or another country in the region.

Of all the ethnic groups in the country, the Tajiks are the mostly mixed and educated group. They have Greek, Arab, Turkic, and other blood in their system. They live mostly in Kabul, Kapisa, Parwan, Panjshir, Badakhshan and are also scattered in Takhar, Konduz, Baghlan, Balkh, Jowzjan, Ghore, and Herat provinces. Unlike the Pashtuns, the Tajiks are non-tribal.

There has always been political and ethnic rivalry between the Tajiks and the Pashtuns. The Tajiks have come to power twice during the last century. In 1929, Habibullah Kalakani took power from King Amanullah for six months, and in 1992, Burhanuddin Rabbani took power from Sebghatullah Mujaddidi. Of all the non-Pashtuns, the Tajiks fought the Taliban until the end. It was the Tajiks who took Kabul from the Taliban in 2001 with assistance from the coalition forces. The primary objective of the Taliban's ethnic cleansing campaign was the Tajiks and their commander Ahmad Shah Massoud.

In the interim and transitional governments of the Karzai government, the Tajiks, especially the Shura-ye Nizar dominated, holding the key ministries. After the presidential elections, however, most of the Tajiks were forced to vacate the key ministries. Currently, even though one of the vice presidents, Ahmad Zia Massoud, and the speaker of parliament, Younis Qanuni, are Tajik, the Pashtuns dominate the three branches of the Afghan government. This may be one of the reasons why a coalition of mostly non-Pashtuns by the name of *jabha-ye milli* (the national front) was created in April 2007. This coalition, led by Burhanudin Rabbani, a Tajik, consists of the former Mujahideen Islamists, Communists, and nationalists, making it, for all intents and purposes, a non-Pashtun front to prevent Pashtun domination. The newly formed front stands for the parliamentary model instead of the existing presidential model of government and wants the provincial governors elected by the residents of each province rather than by the central government. It appears that the Tajiks and other non-Pashtuns are in favor of some type Federalism while the Pashtuns are opposed to it.

The Hazaras

The Hazaras are the third largest ethnic group in Afghanistan comprising of about 17 percent of the total population. They are of mostly Turko-Mongolian origins and reside in what is known as the Hazarajat or Hazaristan (land of the Hazaras) encompassing all of Bamiyan and Dai Kundi provinces and portions of Parwan, Baghlan, Ghazni, Maidan-Wardak, Helmand, and other provinces. There is also a large concentration of Hazaras in Kabul City and Mazar-e Sharif. The most distinctive physical characteristic of the Hazaras are their Mongoloid features—slanted eyes, high cheekbones, and sparse beards.

The Hazaras speak a dialect of Dari called *Hazaragi*. Hazaragi differs from the other dialects of Dari in pronunciation, vocabulary, and syntax. Unlike the other dialects of Dari, Hazaragi has some Mongolian and Turkish vocabulary, but its unique pronunciation is the main difference from other dialects of Dari.

Most Hazaras are Shi'is, but there are also some Sunnis among them. The Shi'i Hazaras are either Imamis/Ithna-Asharis (Twelvers) or Ismailis (Seveners). The latter live in Baghlan province while the former in the Hazarajat proper. According to Mousavi, the Sheikh Ali, Badghisi and Firozkohi Hazaras are Sunni Muslim (Mousavi, 1998:76). Religious ceremonies are held in mosques and Takyakhanas. The latter place of worship is unique to the Shi'is in Afghanistan. Sayids (descendants of the Prophet Mohammad), Mirs, Arbabs, Maliks, and Mullahs are the respected individuals in the Hazara society. The Hazaras also venerate shrines such as *ziaratga* (tombs of holy men) and *nazarga* (sites believed to have been visited by Imams and *Imamzadahs* (descendants of Imams). Some Hazaras also revere irregularly shaped trees.

Not only are Hazaras the most undeveloped political, social, and economic ethnic group, but also the most victimized ethnic group in the country. Until the Communist coup of 1978, Hazaras were mostly excluded from the officer corps of the military and police and were not allowed to become governors, sub-governors, judges, or Afghan ambassadors to foreign countries.

Prior to the invasion of the Soviet Union in 1979 and the subsequent civil war, the Hazara economy was based on agriculture, animal husbandry, and industry. The agricultural crops common in the Hazarajat included mostly wheat, peas, corn, lucerne, and clover. The Hazaras maintained huge live stocks of sheep and sold them to the neighboring provinces. In industry, the Hazarajat was famous for its woolen products such as *barak* (a thick woolen cloth), *gelam* (a type woolen rug, different from the *qalin* (Afghan rug), felt, socks, and gloves.

The Hazaras have been attacked several times by the Pashtun-dominated Afghan governments, taking hundreds and thousands of lives and property. The first was during Abdul Rahman Khan's reign in late nineteenth century. As a result of this attack, thousands of Hazaras had to flee to Pakistan, Iran, and even Central Asia, and their land and pastures were given to the nomadic and sedentary Pashtuns. As a result of such attacks, hundred of Hazara women were brought to Kabul as slaves or servants. It was not until Shah Amanullah (1919-1929) when slavery was banned in the country.

The other big attacks on the Hazarajat took place more recently. One was in 1979 when Hafizullah Amin sent thousands of Pashtun to Bamiyan and killed hundreds of men including boys as young as twelve years of age. The last bloody attack was launched by the Taliban after they came to power, killing Hazaras in Bamiyan, Yakawlang, and other towns in the Hazarajat. This time, the surviving Hazaras fled to Iran and Pakistan and to some provinces such as Balkh and other provinces in the north of the country. Clashes also took place between the Hazaras and the Taliban militia in Mazar-e Sharif.

The Communist coup and the Soviet occupation, however, brought some improvements in the status of Hazaras and other Shi'is politically, socially, and economically in Afghanistan. For the first time in the modern history of the country, a Hazara, Sultan Ali Keshtmand, became prime minister. Hazaras also held other important posts as mayors, governors, military generals, diplomats, and so on. Finally, the Hazaras had their own publications and were allowed to talk about national identity, something that had been taboo during the previous Pashtun governments.

The functioning Hazara/Shi'i political parties in the country include *Hizb-e Wahadat* (Unity Party), led by Karim Khalili, second vice president and *Harakat* (Movement), led by Asef Muhsini. They are Islamist parties who fought against the Soviet occupation as Mujahideens. It is worth noting that Wahdat probably has more Hazaras than Harakat. Members of these parties hold some important posts in the Karzai government, especially in the executive and legislative branches. Another Hazara, Dr. Seema Samar, is a former minister of Women's Affairs and now the head of Afghan Human Rights in Afghanistan. Another Hazara, Dr. Ramazan Bashardoost, formerly minister of planning in the Karzai government and now a member of parliament is very popular not just among the Hazaras but among the Tajiks, especially the residents of Kabul. In fact, it was because of his popularity that the people of the Kabul City elected him for the *Wulusi Jirgah* (the House) in 2006.

The Uzbeks

The fourth largest ethnic group in Afghanistan are the Uzbeks who make up about 9 percent of the population. They speak Uzbeki, a Turkic language, and mostly reside in the northwest (Samangan, Faryab, and Jowzjan). Uzbeki is also spoken natively in Uzbekistan and some regions of Tajikistan. The Uzbeks are said to be descendants of the Central Asian nomadic tribes and adhere to Sunni Islam.

Rashid Dostum is the leader of *Junbish-e Milli* (National Movement) commonly known as Junbish. Dostum was part of the Northern Alliance led by Burhanuddin Rabbani when the Mujahideen came to power after the withdrawal of Soviet troops from Afghanistan and fought the Communist government of Najibullah. But later he switched sides and joined Gulbuddin Hekmatyar's Hizb-e Islami for a while. During the Taliban period, he escaped to Turkey. However, after 9/11, he helped the coalition forces led by the United States to force the Taliban out of the northwest. That is why he does not hold an important post in the Karzai government, and relations between Dostum and Hamid Karzai have not been good. In fact, of all the Afghan ethnic groups, Uzbeks are mostly disenchanted with Hamid Karzai and his government.

ENDNOTES

Introduction

[1] See L. Dupree, *Afghanistan* (1973), for example.
[2] Hofstede, (1980), 18.
[3] Ibid., 13-20.
[4] Hofstede and Hofstede, (2005), 8.
[5] See Hofstede, (1980), 19, for details.
[6] See Ibid, 19 for details.
[7] For more information on these and other introductory concepts on culture, see Hofstede, (1980), 13-23.
[8] *Merriam-Webster's Collegiate Dictionary*, 11th ed., 304.
[9] Hofstede, (1980), 21.
[10] Ibid., 22-23.
[11] Ibid., 21-23.
[12] Hofstede, (1980), 14
[13] In Hofstede and Hofstede, (2005), 207-237, a fifth dimension, *Time Orientation* is added, but it is omitted in this study because it does not seem to be applicable in the Afghan context.

Chapter 1

[14] For more information on the background and details of the concepts mentioned here, see Hofstede, (1980), 65-108.
[15] Hofstede, (1980), 65.
[16] Ibid., 75.

17 Based on the rule of power distance, Marshal Fahim Khan, the former minister of defense in the Karzai government, would have also been called the "Conquer of Kabul" since it was him who captured Kabul from the Taliban in 2001.

18 Arthur Bonner (1987): 80.

19 Hofstede, (1980), 68

20 Myron Weiner and Ali Banuaazizi, eds., "The New Political Elites of Afghanistan," *The Politics of Social Transformation in Afghanistan, Iran and Afghanistan*, 74.

Chapter 2

21 For the details of these and other introductory concepts, see Hofstede, (1980), 110-145.

22 Ibid., 110.

23 See ibid., 122, how other participant countries scored.

24 Hofstede, (1980), 111.

25 Ibid., 138.

26 Ibid, 115-116.

27 Ibid., 138.

28 Ibid., 141-143.

29 The rice we eat is *Baghlani*, from Baghlan, Afghanistan. The same rice is sold in Afghanistan, but it is not clean due to lack of quality control and competition.

30 I am reminded of a conversation I had with one of the Peace Corps trainees a long time ago. When I told him in Afghanistan people dried meat for the winter, he said, "Why don't they freeze it?" He was assuming that because everyone in America has access to electricity and refrigerators, people in the rest of the world do too.

31 Unlike the individualistic societies such as the United States, in Afghanistan, animals are not kept as pets. Of all the animals, dogs and pigs are believed to be the dirtiest. The use of words associated with these for describing people is derogatory and even insulting. Thus, the English sentence,

"He works like a dog," can only be translated as "He works like a donkey." And "he is the company's watchdog" is untranslatable into Dari or Pashto. In Afghanistan, animals must serve a purpose other than companionship. Thus, there are watchdogs and fighting dogs. Similarly, cats in the Afghan households are for the purpose of catching mice, parrots and other birds are for singing and/or fighting. Quails, for example, are kept for both singing and fighting and roosters for fights only. In short, love of animals and keeping them as pets for companionship are often characteristics of individualistic societies such as the United States and other civil and prosperous societies. Thus, if a Westerner has a pet dog or a cat, it is a good idea to keep them outside of the living room when inviting Afghans because they often hate touching dogs and cats, especially the former.

Chapter 3

[32] For background and details on the concepts related to Individualism/Collectivism mentioned here, see Hofstede, (1980): 148-174.

[33] Quoted by Hofstede, (1980),152.

[34] Ibid., 153.

[35] See ibid., 170-174, for additional origins and consequences of collectivism and individualism.

[36] The word *Khurasan* (lit. "east" or "site of the sunrise" in Persian) is the old name used for the region that included parts of modern Iran, Central Asia, modern Afghanistan, and Pakistan prior to the founding of modern Afghanistan in the eighteenth century.

[37] *Omaid Weekly* 16, no. 792, (June 25, 2007): 3.

[38] This is a political issue; ethnic groups exaggerate their percentage in the country. The figures provided here are only estimates provided by foreign sources rather than those claimed by the various ethnic groups.

[39] For more information, see William Maley, 9.

[40] Olivier Roy, "The New Political Elites of Afghanistan," eds. Myron Weiner and Ali Banuazizi, Syracuse: Syracuse University Press, 1994), 74.

[41] Roy Stewart,

[42] Khwaja Bashirahmad Ansari, "The Bleeding Wound of Yakawlang," *Omaid Weekly*, no. 772, (February 5, 2007), 5.

[43] Ghulam Mohammad Ghubar, Vol. 2, 48.

[44] Nazif Shahrani, "Not 'Who' but 'How'?: Governing Afghanistan after the Conflict," *Federations*, (October 2001), 8. *http://www.forumfed.org.*

Chapter 4

[45] For details of the concepts related to MAS paraphrased and summerized here, see Hofstede, (1980), 176-210.

[46] For more information on the nature and measurement of MAS as well as its related concepts and consequences mentioned here, see Hofstede, (1980), 177-210.

[47] The transliteration of the Dari words provided in this study are the spoken form.

[48] Farayba Rafugaran, 7.

[49] Ibid., 12.

[50] The quotations in the literature section are rough English translations. Even in the best translation, some meaning is lost in the process.

[51] Jallal Satari, 101.

[52] Ibid., 102.

[53] Ibid., 102.

[54] Ibid., 111.

[55] Ibid., 115.

[56] Ibid., 112.

[57] Geert Hofstede, 204.

[58] Ibid., 45.

[59] Ibid., 46.

[60] Http://www.rawa.org

[61] Ibid., BBC News, (October 31, 2006).

[62] *www.rawa.org*

[63] "Marriage in Islam," www.jamaat.org

[64] Jalal Satari., 44.

[65] www.rawa.org

[66] Jalal Satari.

[67] Ibid.

[68] Jalal Satari, 38.

[69] Ibid., 83.

[70] The names mentioned here are not the actual names of the people concerned.

[71] *www.rawa.org/womankind*

[72] Ibid.

[73] Ibid.